Live Before You Die

Live Before You Die

Filled with wit, wisdom and insight, this book will give you the opportunity to recognize who you are and who you can be.

Mark M. Hood

Writer's Showcase
San Jose New York Lincoln Shanghai

Live Before You Die
Filled with wit, wisdom and insight, this book will give you
the opportunity to recognize who you are and who you can be.

Writer's Showcase
an imprint of iUniverse, Inc.

For information address:
iUniverse, Inc.
5220 S. 16th St., Suite 200
Lincoln, NE 68512
www.iuniverse.com

Do not read this book if you do not plan on putting the ideas into practice.

ISBN: 0-595-21944-6

Printed in the United States of America

Contents

The Introduction Or, What Is The Point Of This Book?

Originally I wanted to name this book;

"CHICKEN SOUP FOR THE SPIRIT OF DANCING GUARDIAN ANGEL IN MARTHA'S BEAUTIFUL KITCHEN AS SHE IS WATCHING BASEBALL, BAKING AN APPLE PIE FOR HER MOM, ON A BLISSFUL JOURNEY DOWN THE ROAD MOST TRAVELED WITH THE DALAI LAMA, SOUL SEARCHING FOR THE PERFECT MATE OR LEARNING HOW TO FULLY LOVE YOURSELF, AS YOU, AT THE SAME TIME, LEARN TO RECOVER FROM A TROUBLED PAST WHILE EXPERIENCING UNLIMITED FINANCIAL, INTELLECTUAL, EMOTIONAL AND SEXUAL SUCCESS, MASTERING THE SEVEN HABITS OF HIGHLY EFFECTIVE PEOPLE WHO ARE ALWAYS WINNING FRIENDS AND INFLUENCING DYSFUNCTIONAL PEOPLE, AS YOU ARE SALUTING THE AMERICAN FLAG, KEEPING THE WEIGHT OFF BY EATING CHOCOLATE AND MAINTAINING A STRONG MENTAL ATTITUDE THAT WILL TAKE YOU, AND TRULY YOU...OVER THE TOP, DOT COM."

The editor said it would not sell and the publisher said it would never fit on this size front cover. Instead of buying a bigger size, I changed the name.

When asked what I do for a living, and I explain that I majored in psychology and worked in psychiatric hospitals for many the years, invariably people ask me one of two questions, "I have a friend who had a really terrible dream last night. I'll tell you what happened and then you tell me what it means?" or "Isn't it true that people who major in those fields are really hung up on their childhoods, are angry at their parents and then choose a career in which they can help others while they are helping themselves?"

You caught me! I now stand before you totally naked! How do I look?

Actually, the answer is no. But we can all use a little help getting through this thing, don't you think?

I suppose the difference between me and many of my colleagues is that I don't believe it's a psychologist's or psychiatrist's job to hold someone's hand so much as to give them a hand. Thus, my notion of a self-help book may be a radical departure from that of the thousands of other books on the market.

My notion of a self-help book is two-fold: 1) that, while therapy is a good thing, and I recommend it highly as part of a balanced breakfast and all that, most likely you're not as neurotic as you think or as mass-market psychobabble books seem to insinuate, and 2) self-help should be just that: self help.

I suggest the following paradox (as opposed to a "pair of docs," which most HMO's won't cover anyway): This is not a self-help book in the traditional sense of the term; yet, in my thinking, it may be the first true self-help book out there, in that I hope it creates an environment for you – perhaps for the first time in your life – to truly help yourself.

What is the reason for writing such a book?

From the dawn of humankind to the prehistoric madmen, shamans, priests, doctors, TV evangelists, psychics, game show hosts and anyone who has a desire to relieve the human condition of pain and suffering, we are all in search of the secret to happiness or to simply lessen our present state of discomfort. The promise of a miraculous cure, in countless forms, has been claimed to be the missing element to relieve people from their pain and glide them back to comfort. This overwhelming desire pulls people to do and try some strange things — from the fantasy of holding the multimillion-dollar lottery ticket to soaking in tubs of healing mud.

From the field of psychology to over-the-counter self-help, it all follows the same line only with different approaches. Why is it that everyone seems to be reaching for something that may already exist within him or her? We have become a society of self-improvers with little or no contentment and appreciation for who we are and what we have. It can always be just a little better than what it is now, and we demand it. When confronted with a personal problem, we tend to grasp for the new pop mantra, technique or electrical gadget to take care of it. It has become commonplace to have discussion about our recent psychosomatic disorder and cabinet-full of pills to define how much stress we are all under. Our lives have become gradually more pressured, attempting to do as much as possible with less time to accomplish it all. Americans of all ages are becoming more alienated, working harder and sleeping less. We have all become hungrier for the secret ingredient for stress relief, balance, success, love and contentment. Many of these magic elixirs come in the form of an incredible, never-before-uncovered concept that will be the panacea for all our ills.

Oops, it doesn't work — again!

With the complex nature of the human condition, how is it that these self-help gurus of the cure can eradicate your ills by a simple formula? But there is no simple formula. If there were, you'd be bumping into a mass of happy humanity that would now be roaming the Earth completely fulfilled. To this point, anyway, society has yet to be overrun by such creatures.

It is my hope that this book will delightfully surprise you. It will push you to look beyond what you have been doing, and how you have been thinking, and to begin to reach for the deeper answers to your perplexing questions. The thoughts within this book will help you to reach that state of aliveness.

I'm not saying it will be easy or painless. In any endeavor that seeks to improve one's position in any permanent way, there is going to be some amount of exertion or even discomfort. Yet, perhaps due to disingenuous, feel-good marketing, there is a strong belief that any type of psychological or physiological discomfort is bad or undesirable. Therefore, with enough work through our will/thinking/treatment, our present condition will become more tolerable — which leads us to believe that there is no value in a crisis or discomfort or pain. Is it necessary that we continuously find a quick remedy to alleviate all of our suffering? Of course not! Fact is, not all pain is bad. Sometimes precisely the thing to do is to lean into the proverbial left hook.

Maybe we should take George Bernard Shaw's recommendation from "Man and Superman": "A lifetime of happiness! No man alive could bear it: it would be hell on Earth."

Nietzsche once wrote, "He who would learn to fly one day must first learn to stand and walk and run and climb and dance; one cannot fly into flying." All positive change will take time and persistence in order for it to remain a lasting character trait. So, the beauty behind the search for optimism is that it is a continuous learning process. Not one-stop shopping, but experimenting and testing with the multitude of potential resources. It is a lifetime learning process that requires continuous work on our part.

We can make significant changes in our lives, certainly. But most lasting and desirable change will require time and work on our part; patience is required to reach whatever destination we have chosen. One cannot simply will oneself across the ocean. Our society of armchair pseudo-therapists who shout out "Hey, why don't you just get over it?" are in no way encouraging supportive change for someone in search of answers. They're trying to sell you sweet-tasting elixirs. Oh, sure, each spoonful may give you a momentary sugar high, but when the glucose wears off, you're on your own.

I offer you no such magic elixirs – rather, the magic of self-discovery, and, as a result, true self help. I offer you a book full of ideas, with a mixture of psychology as well as personal experiences. I offer you a road map to whatever destination you seek. Self-help is a process, not a pill. After all, isn't that the best of psychology – the freedom to stitch your own tapestry of life?

This is not a textbook filled with high-minded academic jargon, but more of a personal essay on this bewildering condition called "being human." I trust these writings will prove in a small, but profound, way that, contrary to much of what you've previously read and been told, most of the supplies you need to make your life's journey are already on board. They're inside you. All you really need is to know where to look. There is a strength and a love and a fire in your soul that, once relit, will light your way.

I begin each chapter with an inspiring quote or two, and a dramatic photograph, to set the tone and convey the chapter's overall theme. This is the result of a combination of my love for both the pithy aphorism and the drama of photography (especially black and white), as well the realization that words can, at times, be happily subjugated to the beauty, power and artistry of the visual art.

The chapters of this book were created from a series courses and speeches I have given over the years. Originally the topics involved mental illness. I believed my mission, at the time, was to remind people that they were actually sicker than they imagined. Maybe this was supposed to be good for business. After a time, I switched to more health-related issues. I saw that people were in search of health rather than illness. I also believe that we are all a little neurotic about our human condition and need to be reminded that it's O.K. to be less than perfect.

It is my hope you would use the various chapters of this book as signposts along the journey to health, wholeness and happiness. You have the ability to take any detour along the way, because, as you already know, you are in complete control.

And you don't need as much help as you think.

ACKNOWLEDGEMENTS

This is to my patient, lovely and talented wife, Melissa, who waited a year for this cathartic project to finally come to an end.

All the boys in the house; Aaron, Ryan and Charles.

A brilliantly gifted editor who needs very little inspiration and encouragement. Michael Ryan was able to weave my tangential thoughts into a masterpiece of comprehensible words. I am puzzled why he hasn't won the Pulitzer Prize yet. Oh, that's right, he has to be nominated first!

David Eulitt, with the award-winning photographs from someone who has truly found his bliss in life. There were also additional photos from Michael and myself.

My parents, for giving me life, and my brothers and sisters who continue to enhanced it.

Everyone, and you know who you are, who has influenced my thinking and actions throughout my life.

And the never-ending input from my introverted, intuitive, analytical research assistant who kept me straight with all the facts and details that were so essential to the completion of this book.

The primary inspiration behind the writing of this book was to give the finished manuscript as a gift to my son, Aaron. The gift was given as he left to spend a year in Japan as a high school foreign exchange student. I am sure he will recognize some of my thoughts as lessons I have tried to teach him.

CHAPTER 1

Being positive really isn't that easy — or is it?

"Don't sweat the petty stuff and don't pet the sweaty stuff."

We come into this world so full of potential. As we develop, some of us come to the same realization that Woody Allen did: that "life is full of miserableness, loneliness, suffering, unhappiness and it's all over much too quickly."

Maybe this is true! Since 1960 the divorce rate has doubled to over 50%, teen suicide has tripled, violent crimes have quadrupled, the prison population has quintupled and it is estimated that the incidence of depression is ten times what it was in the 1900s.

We are growing up in an epidemic of depression. Reports indicate that each of us experiences 7 to 10 depressive episodes a year serious enough to reach out for professional assistance.

One of the strongest factors influencing this depression is a sense of pessimism. Contrary to our national self-image of blissful happiness, our epidemic of depression among *all* ages shows that we are at serious risk of becoming a culture of pessimists.

Pessimism becomes an ingrained habit of seeing the bad events — the weather, the economy, crime, and moral decline — as pervasive and permanent. The optimist has the skill of finding temporary causes and hopeful solutions to these very same events. The greatest of all optimists

1

is the person who proclaims we live in the best of worlds. The pessimist fears that such is true.

It is the irony of our times that, although we are more tolerant of one another than previous generations, we trust each other less. We continue to turn to the courts and law enforcement to make others keep their word, or to punish them when they don't.

Pessimism is not an inborn genetic blueprint — we learn it from our parents, siblings, teachers and mentors, as well as those with whom we choose to associate. Call it the high cost of loathing: Pessimism is a way of being and behaving that has enormous costs. For individuals it can produce hopelessness that leads to depression, lowered work productivity and overall poor health (spiritual, mental and physical). Multiplied across a family, peers, work mates, communities and nations, it produces a vacuum all its own — and it will surely suck you in.

I have always said that there is an extremely large gap between knowing and doing. Words are meaningless unless followed by strong actions.

You would think that optimism would be easy. Optimistic people certainly make it appear so! Truth is, though, becoming positive in this world at times appears to be a constant battle. Sadly enough, sometimes the slightest setbacks can cause one to fall into an abyss of depression. Well-laid plans are set off course and the individual begins to focus in on only the negative effects. Experiences are viewed as black and white, negative or positive. And inescapably, it seems, it is the negative that exhibits the greatest gravitational pull. It just drags you down.

All the attention the media give to the evil and ill will of our society can place one in a continuous state of doom and gloom. It will be a struggle to maintain a positive focus. But rest assured, it is a *choice*. Tragically, I believe we are socialized – actually encouraged by society — to gravitate toward the negative, *not* the positive. Thus, you're not only fighting gravity yourself in order to maintain a positive outlook, you're battling the crushing weight of others as well.

Most likely, that perverse attraction of ours to the negative has something to do with our training in childhood and the fact that most of the reinforcement we received occurred when we stepped out of line, rather than staying within the line of conformity. I have put together a condensed list of recommendations for changing your inner conditions into a healthier, more optimistic outlook on the world. You must first be aware of the countless obstacles that will block you. I have listed a few of the most common reasons people use to stop themselves from growth and change: I would love to change, but I live in (your city here); I'm too old; I need more money; I need more time; I'm married; I'm not married yet; I'm divorced; I have children; you have no idea what traumas I had as a child/adolescent/adult; it's those politicians (caution: this one may be true!); I'm working through another crisis right now; I have sinned; I never get any of the great breaks in life; I have persistent hair problems and/or weight problems; I have too many responsibilities right now; it's my job; I'm waiting for the weather to change first. My favorite existential explanation is that I'm quite comfortable living this life of quiet desperation.

Certainly, a deprived childhood, abusive people, poverty, and a host of other very good and real reasons over which one has little or no control may make it difficult for an individual to be optimistic in life. At the same time, there are countless examples of those who have overcome unbelievable tragedies and hurdles and have concluded that whatever happens on the outside does not have to have a lasting detrimental effect on the inside. Such people confront the tragedy, respect its place in their lives and then immerse themselves in whatever endeavors they choose to work on, toward whatever goal they choose. Talk about empowerment!

The prospects for good health and lifelong resilience are remarkably dependent upon your learned mental habits. Your attitudes are directly related to your emotional reactions, which strongly affect your immune system, circulatory system and even risk for accidents.

The strength of this relationship between attitudes and health has been grossly underestimated. In 1973, Dr. Grossarth-Maticek gave a brief test measuring habitual feelings of pleasure and well being among thousands of senior residents in Heidelberg, Germany. Twenty-two years later, the test scores were compared with health status. The 300 people who had scored highest turned out to be 30 times more likely to be alive and well 21 years later than the 200 lowest. The test focused only on mental factors, yet, astoundingly, it predicted future health more effectively than traditional tests on well-known risk factors such as genetics, lifestyle, smoking and diet. Think of what that says about your own health! In a nutshell, much of your present and future health is a function of your attitude!

I really love reading longitudinal studies to find out the secret ingredients to mental health and emotional well-being. I get exceptionally excited when I am constantly reminded of the "against the normal mindset thinking" studies. In particular, the studies demonstrating that major life events, such as getting married and experiencing the death of a loved one have little influence on long-term satisfaction and well-being. In fact, lottery winners are not happier than others. If they were miserable before, they will remain that way in spite of all the money they receive. The overwhelming finding is that well being is determined by individual characteristics, *not* external circumstances. Unhappy people haven't experienced any more bad luck than happy people. Someday I plan to test that finding by winning the lottery and seeing if I can somehow remain happy!

We'll explore all this in depth later, but for now here's a quick rundown of some of what you can do in order to pull away from the gravitational pull of pessimism:

> Constantly remind yourself that being positive is a choice that only you can make for yourself.

> ➤ Look at every *crisis* as an opportunity for growth and development.
> ➤ Become the ultimate athlete.
> ➤ Don't make work a four-letter word.
> ➤ Find the best way to become relaxed.
> ➤ Associate with the right people.
> ➤ Check your aphorisms and self-destructive dialogue.
> ➤ Pump up your belief system.
> ➤ Dare to be different and try something exciting.
> ➤ You are not alone.
> ➤ Quit trying to understand the opposite sex.
> ➤ Learn or re-learn how to laugh, especially at yourself.
> ➤ A high self-esteem is great if can also be humble.
> ➤ Giving to others benefits you as much as them.
> ➤ Power and success require, above all, character.
> ➤ When you've got *it*, you know *it*!

Why is it that we gravitate so strongly toward the negative? Are we wired up in a way that promotes this type of pull toward the pessimistic point of view? In a word, yes. We trained at a young age to respond more attentively when someone points out the negative or raises their voice in order to gain our attention. Negative imprinting has become a more powerful influence on changing our actions, much more so than positive reinforcers. It was P.D. Ouspensky who said, "The strangest and most fantastic fact about negative emotions is that people actually worship them."

If you can change your underwear...then you can change your attitude!

Of course, for most of us, changing our underwear is relatively simple. (If you're not one of those people, you might consider reading instead, "Dressing for Dummies.") In contrast, changing one's attitude takes more thought.

The first step is to answer the question of where your attitude comes from.

There are basically two sources for one's attitude: external and internal. All of us, to one extent or another, are buffeted by external events and stimuli. The real question is how much control you allow external happenings – i.e., the world around you – to control your attitude and, therefore, control you.

What we're talking about here is nothing less than your frame of reference for understanding the world and how you fit in it, your interpretation of life. Those who are driven by a strong internal sense of control – a feeling that they are in control of their feelings and attitudes and responses to the world – are able to exude a sense of stability, a command over their kingdom as it were. The picture they paint is that they are not out of control even when the outer world seems out of control.

Conversely, those who allow themselves to be controlled an inordinate amount by external factors – how the boss treated them today, the awful driver in front of them, even the weather – almost merge with the environment. They take on the mood of the world around them. They cede control of their lives to the vagaries of fate, bouncing from mood-producing event to mood-producing event like a pinball seemingly controlled by nothing more than chance (or a hapless drunk working the flippers). It's a sad fate, and hardly necessary. Holocaust survivor Viktor Frankl found that even in a concentration camp, where his captors were determining everything about his life, including its very existence, he could seize control of his attitude. It was the only thing they could not take from him.

You are no different, and certainly no less powerful. The extent of control you have over your world can be boiled down to your sense of control, internal versus external. How much inner control you possess will determine how well you will be able to adjust and adapt to the outer world.

All of us fall somewhere on a continuum between external and internal controls. Our view of the world – down to whether we consider ourselves to have had a good day or a bad day – depends upon the degree to which we are powered by internal goals and desires versus the degree by which they are controlled by external social reinforcers.

It will influence absolutely everything in your life, most notably your level of optimism.

Ask yourself right now which thought process you lean toward most often, externally driven or internally driven. With an internal locus of control, you believe that an event in the outside world, whatever it may be, is contingent upon your own behavior. You are more likely to believe you can influence the outcome of whatever is going on around you. So you are more likely to be proactive and positive in your actions.

An individual with an external locus of control relies more on the fate, really — the control of others. The externally driven are actively trying to learn and adjust to the societal rules, becoming more of a conformist. They gain most of their clues from the outside field rather than internal feedback. Their actions are viewed as luck, chance or fate rather than something they have generated. Most of the control is outside of the individual.

This isn't magic, but the result of it can be: You need to learn to see the big picture when it comes to maintaining optimism and not sweating the small stuff. Such people are the unique individuals who are able to observe, process, place things in a larger scheme and then readjust their actions.

It is the greatest of our God given freedoms to "BE" our attitude in any situation!

Norman Cousins, in "Anatomy Of An Illness As Perceived By The Patient," said, "I have learned never to underestimate the capacity of the human mind to regenerate — even when the prospects seem most wretched. The life force may be the least understood force on Earth. William James said that human beings tend to live far within self-imposed limits. It is possible that these limits will recede when we respect more fully the natural drive of the human mind and body toward perfectibility and regeneration. Protecting and cherishing that natural drive may well represent the finest exercise of human freedom."

In other words, we all possess a wonderful, beautiful, incredible capacity for resiliency – the ability to bounce back from adversity stronger than anyone believed possible. Truly, it is a natural process – otherwise, we would all be paralyzed for life with sorrow after our first great loss. The trick is to create the frame of mind for that process to take hold. You force yourself to get out of bed when you feel you can't go on. You face your greatest fears or failures head-on. You simply determine to take one step and then another – and pretty soon you realize you're walking again. Before long, you're flying again.

Remember: That capacity is within us all. It needs only to be allowed to take place. In allowing the wisdom of the mind to bounce back from adversity, to shut out the noise from outside and to give in to the strength of our pre-programmed internal drive, you open yourself up to achieving levels of health and understanding you never dreamed possible.

Abraham Maslow said, "If the only tool you have is a hammer, you tend to treat everything as if it were a nail." We need and have more tools at our disposal than just a hammer, so let's get into the tool shed now – and start work on constructing a new you.

CHAPTER 2

The anatomy of self-destructiveness

"An unexamined life is not worth living."
Thoreau

Even though Thoreau made this statement for our increasingly cerebral society it is equally true that *"ignorance is bliss."*

Many people, at times, feel awful, miserable and sick. We live our lives on an ever-changing continuum, ranging from optimal health to the depths of severe sickness. While it is true that most people have not consciously chosen this road to sickness, I submit that we set the stage with our own internal unhealthy dialogue.

We can call these ingrained thought patterns unrealistic expectations or just plain stinkin' thinkin'. This is our internal communication/dialogue that is constantly working. It is the continuous talking we do to ourselves in our evaluations of others and ourselves.

The main issue in our level of sanity is not whether we talk to ourselves; we all do. It is more important *how* we talk to ourselves. The usual joke is that crazy people answer themselves when they talk to themselves. Well, the joke is a reality, except the part about being crazy. We all talk to ourselves and answer these questions — questions concerning our adequacy, how we fit into the world, how the world perceives our acts and more.

Where we run into a problem is when our inner voice is unnecessarily negative and self-critical – and, therefore, self-limiting.

10

Below are 13 ways in which we set ourselves up for failure through a type of repetitive pessimistic internal dialogue:

> *We learn during early childhood to adapt, form habits, become stuck, resist change, become defensive, and then self-righteous because there is only one way to do it, and it is MY WAY!* This is, in part, the belief that the strong influence of our past will create the destiny for our future. Even though this is partially true, we tend to forget about the unlimited possibilities that await us all.

> *We live only on a superficial level of awareness,* basing impressions solely on external appearance because it is true that "all that glitters is gold" and it is more important, as Billy Crystal's character would say, to look good than to feel good, darling. In reality, the more you talk with an individual, the closer you connect and find that there are many depths beyond the superficial front.

> *We remain on the road most traveled.* Stepping outside of our comfort zone and attempting new adventures would cause too much disruption in our balanced lives. Staying stuck in the rut and remaining unchallenged will reinforce Thoreau's famous statement that, "Most men lead lives of quiet desperation."

> *We maintain self-restraint and extreme rigidity.* The goal of stress management is the ability to reach the state of resiliency and flexibility. Research has shown that the more psychologically and physiologically rigid you become, the greater the possibility that you will "snap."

> *We develop a people- pleasing personality.* We – and women are really guilty of this — get trapped into believing that the main goal of a human is to ensure that all those around you are happy and fulfilled. If there is disorder, you are somehow responsible and need to do something in order to change the

disruption. This trap will drive you nuts, and likely those around you. Don't fall into it. A sign of maturity is the realization that you are responsible for your own moods and have very limited power over others. Feel for others, certainly. Empathize, sympathize and act with love and compassion. But as Deepak Chopra noted, if you take on someone else's pain (or mood, I'd add), all you've done is doubled it.

➤ *We shun any and all types of humor.* This world is far too serious a place to be funny in, right? WRONG, therapy breathe! Yes, humor must have its place, but it's a much roomier place than most sad souls allow. Give others the space to be a little inappropriate at times. And dare to do it yourself. Don't forget what Josh Billings said "There ain't much fun in medicine, but there's a heck of a lot of medicine in fun."

➤ *We always blame others and abstain from any personal responsibility.* Here's a radical thought for you: It's not always someone else's fault. It's not always *anyone's* fault. Two things happen when you accept responsibility: Those around you respect you for it, and you wisely take yourself out of the no-win blame game.

➤ *We display a sense of entitlement and narcissism, or extreme self-love.* We somehow come to believe that the world really does revolve around us, and that all of these people have been placed here to satisfy all of our needs. While that is true at some of your finer hotels and restaurants, it's not at all true in the world at large. Yet, we become angry or depressed when we don't always get our way *(I am special! Don't these people know who I am?)*. Here's a real shock for you: A narcissistic personality doesn't work for anyone after the age of 2. Grow up!

➤ *We "should" ourselves to death for not being perfect.* If you can't do something and achieve perfect results, then don't do it at all, we tell ourselves (whether we realize it or not). We get it in our head that we're all born to achieve the highest of goals and that nothing less than the absolute best will be tolerated. Wow! Give yourself a break, for goodness' sake! Chances are, you're doing a lot better than you will ever give yourself credit for. And life teaches us that the greatest success comes after countless failures.

➤ *We cling onto things because whoever dies with the most toys wins.* We become caught up with the consumer mentality and it becomes the way others view our external appearance of identity and "success." At the end of the game, who you are matters more than what you have. Shouldn't it instead be "Whoever dies with the most *joys* wins"?

➤ *We constantly compare ourselves to others.* You figure if you don't achieve the same or greater "success" as others, you are obviously less than adequate, so you should act as such. Two problems here: First, what's your definition of success? Second, why on God's green Earth should you care how you're doing vis-à-vis someone else? Why do should you seek to be like others when you're pretty doggone nice yourself? And if you feel compelled to compare yourself to something, how about comparing yourself to how you started out? Or to your ultimate goals in life? Wouldn't that be a heck of a lot more instructive, as well as constructive?

➤ *We keep people away and resist intimacy.* An increasing distrust of others tends to occur when you've experienced the agony of betrayal or the pain of lost love. Intimacy and love require a lot of courage and a renewed desire to try again.

➤ *We deny the present moment by dwelling on the past and being anxious about the future.* As in a casino, when it comes to life, "You must be present to win." We spend the majority of our conscious moments chained to the past or in fearful anticipation of the future. Many forms of prayer and meditation ultimately teach us to concentrate on each and every precious moment. Someone once said, "Yesterday is history, tomorrow is a mystery and today is a gift – that's why they call it the present." Being in the here and now – soaking up every bit of joy from your surroundings – is one of the greatest gifts you'll ever give yourself.

Be aware of these traps your inner voice has been programmed to set for you. They will trip you up. Avoiding them is the first careful step in your journey toward lasting change. Keep in mind the Chinese proverb, *"Small changes bring big rewards."*

"Our life is what our thoughts make it."
Marcus Aurelius Antonius

CHAPTER 3

I may not be much, but I'm all I ever think about

(The thin line between high self-esteem and narcissism)

"Don't be humble; you're not that great"
GOLDA MIER

When the new patient arrives and settles comfortably on the analyst's couch, the psychiatrist begins the initial therapy session.

"Now, I'm not aware of your presenting problem," the doctor softly says. "So perhaps you should start at the beginning."

Why of course," replied the patient. "Well, in the beginning, on the first day, I created the Heavens and Earth…"

This is the type of person who is extremely hard to deal with.

A person enters into a social encounter and spends the entire time talking about what a wonderful, talented, brilliant and successful person he is. Just before the required time elapses, he turns to the other person and says, "Well enough about me; what do *you* think of *me*?"

This form of self-love was perfectly exemplified in Mack Davis' hit song, "Hard To Be Humble":

> "Oh Lord, it's hard to be humble
> When you're perfect in every way

I can't wait to look in the mirror
'Cause I get better lookin' each day
To know me is to love me
I must be a hell of a man
Oh Lord, it's hard to be humble
But I'm doin' the best that I can."

We train our children and attempt to develop positive self-esteem, but there appears to be a rising sense of entitlement and narcissism.

These people, the egotists, are without a doubt, the most difficult individuals to relate to. It is as if adulation must be filled into a psychic container within them that will never fill up. They will never be complete because their needs are so great. No, wait a minute, *they* are so great! Just give them a few minutes and they will tell you how wonderful they are.

Something goes terribly wrong somewhere in the development of that kind of precious ego. It's either too much or too little stimulation, but wires and self-esteem get tangled up and you have a raging egocentric fool — one who is so consumed with his external gratification that no one else exists, except for his own need to feed his self-worth.

You can see it in our leaders, in the boardroom, in politics, experience it in the corporate world; you see it in mating behavior, at the local athletic facility, in star athletes and musicians, and when someone goes overboard to prove his power. Narcissism can be viewed on the roads, standing in the checkout line, or anytime someone isn't getting his way. We are moving into an age in which so many people have become so self-consumed with their own inflated importance that it is becoming more difficult for us to co-exist.

These people also have accompanying anger outbursts, primarily because they feel as if they are not recognized as much as they should be or they don't get their way all of the time.

According to the Greek myth, Narcissus was a handsome young Thespian with whom the nymph Echo fell in love. Echo had been deprived of speech by Hera, the wife of Zeus, and could only repeat the last syllables of words she heard. Unable to express her love for Narcissus, she was rejected by him and died of a broken heart. The gods then punished Narcissus for his callous treatment of Echo by making him fall in love with his own image. It had been predicted by the prophet Tiresias that Narcissus would live until he saw himself. One day while he was leaning over the limpid waters of a fountain, Narcissus caught sight of his own reflection in the water. He became passionately enamored of his image and refused to leave the spot. He died of stagnation and turned into a flower — the narcissus that grows at the edges of springs.

Similarly, when we become self-absorbed, we stagnate. We don't learn from those around us, because we figure they have nothing they can teach us. It's a delicate balance: You need to love yourself without falling *in* love with yourself.

When one's self-esteem gets out-of-control!

It was Eleanor Roosevelt who once stated, "No one can make you feel inferior without your consent." I will add that, "Only you can make you feel omnipotent with your consent."

Narcissists have an exaggerated perception of self-importance. They exaggerate their accomplishments and talents, and expect to be noticed as "special" even without achievement. They often feel that because of their "specialness," their problems are unique, and can be understood only by other special people (the chosen few). Frequently this sense of self-importance alternates with deeper feelings of unworthiness and depression.

These people are obsessed with ungrounded thoughts of unlimited success, power, brilliance, strength, beauty, or ideal love, and with exaggerated feelings of envy for those whom they perceive as being more prominent than they are. These fantasies frequently substitute for realistic activity, when such goals are actually pursued; it is often a blindly driven, pleasure less ambition that will never be satisfied.

Ironically, despite the ornate façade of self worth, narcissists' self-esteem is very fragile. These individuals may be preoccupied with how well they are doing and how well others regard them in their performance. This often takes the form of an almost exhibitionistic need for constant attention and admiration, so look at me! They constantly fish for compliments to feed their ego, often with great charm. In response to criticism, he/she may react with rage, shame, or humiliation, but mask these feelings with an aura of cool indifference. Close relationships are invariably disturbed. What others have to offer is not valued and often underestimated. They continue to long for the admiration of those who have yet to recognize their "greatness." "If you only knew me and my special-ness, you would come to appreciate my greatness!"

A lack of empathy toward others is common. A sense of entitlement— an unreasonable expectation of especially favorable treatment — is usually present. If they lack it, how can they give it?

Friendships are often made only after the person considers how he/she can profit from them, and often leaves after getting what was needed. Their mode of operation is that of exploitation of the other. There is an uncomfortable emotional coldness that is felt, and a disregard for the others' view of the world. After they have withdrawn as much as possible to feed their self-interest, they are on to the next victim. Unless, of course, the victim chooses to stay, and in some way would benefit from this type of bizarre interpersonal relationship. In this type of unhealthy bond, the victim has the difficult job of holding up the mirror to the narcissist in order for them to be admired.

Thus, in many ways, a narcissist is a psychological predator, preying on unwitting – and sometimes unwittingly compliant – victims. They feed off the warm flesh of perceived adulation or accomplishment. The victim, perhaps without knowing it, is harmed by having his own sense of worth gutted. Be on the lookout for narcissists in the tall grass and avoid them – or learn how to ward them off.

Here are some character traits of the narcissist to help you identify this psychological predator:

Condescending
Patronizing
Greater-than-thou
Snobbishness
Arrogance
Haughty
Lack of empathy/compassion
Always using "I" statements
Pulling the conversation back to them
Exploitation

As far as a leadership trait, narcissism is the most ineffective and destructive tool an individual can display. It is a strange phenomenon in our culture that leadership, at times, breeds a Narcissus to fill this position. It is very unfortunate for those who are following them, as well as those who must live with them.

So, what does all this mean for you?

The best one can do when dealing with narcissists is to recognize their symptoms. Do not seek to change their behavior, because it is their responsibility to take that change on. The probability that they will seek change is slight, because this would require a lot of time and a lot of introspective pain on their part. Remember, what we are dealing with in a narcissist is an underlying feeling of worthlessness, and who wants to re-experience that feeling? Only a sadomasochist!

In the end, an innocent victim of narcissistic personalities can become exhausted if he tires to feed them with all their needed ego reassurance.

Understand that their needs are deep and may never be fulfilled — and it's not your job to do it anyway. Just recognize the trap the narcissists have set for you, make the conscious choice to leave the situation, move on, and hope they are forced to join an NA group (Narcissists Anonymous). I understand that attendance is very low at these meetings – though a good time is had by all.

Upon partial completion of this section, my brilliant and introverted research assistant had an interesting observation. She said that all of this stuff about the self-centered personality is good and fine, but how does one deal with them? Especially if I am alluding to the fact that we are breeding more and more of these types all the time. She began to laugh when I suggested a long reading list.

So, I said here are some thoughts to ponder when dealing with a megalomaniac. The best that one can do when dealing with these individuals is to recognize their symptoms. Do not seek to change them because it is their responsibility to take that change on. The probability that they will seek change is slight, because this would require a lot of introspective pain on their part. Remember what we are dealing with here is an underlying feeling of worthlessness, and who wants to re-experience that feeling? Maybe a sadomasochist!

In the end, the recipient of a narcissistic personality can become exhausted if they try to feed him/her with all of their needed energy. You need to understand that their needs are deep and will probably never be fulfilled.

You may have to make the conscious to leave the situation/relationship when you have reached your predetermined level of pain.

One other recommendation I have is to make a copy of this chapter and place it, anonymously, in a place where they will be sure to find it: *Taped to the mirror!*

One of the best ways to enhance your self-esteem is to begin to see the big picture of the world through others, not merely yourself. The eyes of poor self-esteem, and the sound of an overly critical inner voice, perceive the condescension and self-important blithering of a narcissist as someone who is better than they are. But if you have a solid sense of self, and the wisdom to use external means to recognize a narcissist when you see and hear one, you'll know that the condescension that comes your way says absolutely nothing about you. It says a lot, rather, about the self-absorbed, insecure blowhard you're dealing with.

> ## The goal of all humans is to reach a high level of self-acceptance, but with an equally powerful mixture of humility.

Healthy individuals feel good about themselves and are confident in their abilities to cope with what the world throws at them. They will suffer the slings and arrows of human misfortunes, but through a mature developmental process, they learn from their failures.

The personality theorist Erik Erikson proposes that we all face a specific psychosocial dilemma, or "crisis," at each stage of life. More about this later!

Ways to decrease as well as increase one's self-esteem

LOW SELF-ESTEEM COMES FROM

Being ignored   Being disrespected   Neglect
Abuse
Prejudice   Not being taken   seriously
Not being listened to
Put Downs   Criticism   Humiliation
Labeling   Unkind comparisons   Perfectionism

HIGH SELF-ESTEEM COMES FROM

Love   Respect   Trust   Attention
Acceptance   Affection   Belonging
Being believed in   Encouragement   Play   Laughter

Buddhists say, "Act as if the future of the universe depended on what you did, while laughing at yourself for thinking that whatever you do makes any difference." The narcissist truly believes in the first part of this statement, but not the latter. You will be happier and healthier, almost overnight, if you truly believe both parts.

Note: If you're intellectually honest enough to have seen some of yourself in the description of narcissistic behavior, congratulations! You're even better than you thought!
Still, maybe you ought to work on getting over yourself a bit by reading Chapter 4 – preferably in a room without a mirror!

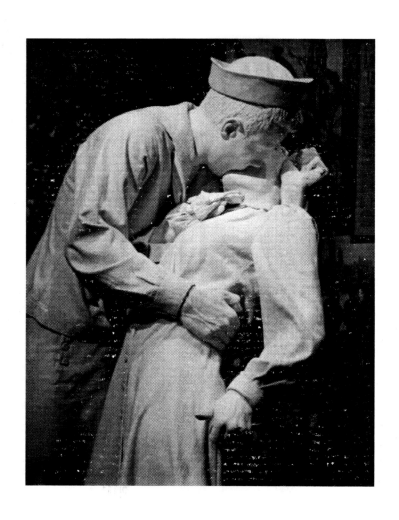

CHAPTER 4

Altruism, benevolence and unselfish acts.

"No act of kindness, no matter
how small, is ever wasted." Aesop

*"The fruit of love is service, which is compassion in action. Religion
has nothing to do with compassion; it is love for God that is the main
thing because we have all been created for the sole purpose to love and
be loved."*
Mother Teresa

*"So long as we love we serve;
so long as we are loved by others,
I would almost say we are indispensable;
and no man is useless while he has a friend."*
Robert Louis Stevenson

"Life's most persistent and urgent question is:
What are you doing for others?"
Dr. Martin Luther King, Jr.

Altruism is the practice of unselfish concern for the welfare of others, as opposed to egoism or the narcissism discussed in the last chapter. If I am an altruist, I am more concerned about others than myself. Altruism is a realization of the importance of harmony with others and service to others. There are obvious benefits to the receiver of the act of giving, but the internal benefits of giving are just as strong, if not stronger.

We can summarize giving as a great act of love — love on one of several human levels. The act of helping others many times comes in the form of charitable contributions to a particular cause or organization. These monetary gifts are beneficial and necessary, but I want to focus on the actual one-on-one act of giving. The contribution of money is one form of kindness, but it pales in comparison to the eye-to-eye human contact that flows from the love of one another.

The presence that people generate creates energy that is therapeutic for all involved.

In other words, your very existence is a gift to others, and makes a huge impact on the world. Knowing that, how could you ever have a bad day? And how could you ever look at yourself or others the same again?

Narcissism need not be taught; in many ways, we're all born to be narcissists. Love for others can be taught, however, and must be. The most effective way of teaching love and compassion is through acts of kindness toward others – i.e., setting an example of selflessness and love. Words are not enough; they are limiting and are useless unless put into practice. But when love of others is put into action, what a great way of developing a lasting character trait in a soul void of empathy for others. And what a world we would create if everyone were operating from this starting point.

The greatest gift you will ever be able to give another is the compassion of your time. This act can be reduced to an act of pure love.

When an individual is in a state of depression or hopelessness, it becomes all too common for them to isolate themselves from others. One of the paths to overcome this state of despair is to go beyond yourself and be with others. Taken one step further, not only to be with others, but also to help others. One small act of compassion can go along way for the well-being of a life out of balance.

Several years ago I read an amazing finding directed related to a form of love. As the human body ages, many physical maladies begin to occur. It has been shown that the majority of health care dollars are spend in the last few years of an individuals' life. Several studies have shown that by simply introducing a small pet (dog, cat, rabbit, birds, etc.) into a retirement or nursing home environment, there is a dramatic reduction in the number of times the residents call their physicians. Is it because of the smell of these creatures? Maybe the noises they make? In reality, it is the unconditional love that is being transmitted to and from this pet that is the secret element. It is amazing how simple this is. The end result is the ability to express a passion that had been dormant for so long.

Everyone who is able to should own a pet. They are little emotion sponges. They exist to absorb the emotions of those around them. When they reach the saturation point, the emotion drips back to the human giver. The human companion is thus doubly blessed – first, by the ability to share unconditional love with that furry or feathery little thing, then to have that love flowing right back.

There is a strong correlation to having a pet to strengthen your immune system. In the end, it is the stimulation of the experience of love. Maybe pets should take on the unofficial role of therapist? I would just be a little confused about how they would do the billing to the insurance company!

"It is this intangible thing, love, love in many forms, which enters into every therapeutic relationship. It is an element of which the

physician may be the carrier, the vessel. And it is an element which binds and heals, which comforts and restores, which works what we have to call—for now—miracles."
Karl Menninger, The Vital Balance

When we speak of love, let us not reduce it to single act or feeling. There are countless avenues for the expression of our love. The ancient Greeks' definition of love differentiates among five types:

EROS-Romantic   *PHILIA*-Friendship   *LUDE*-Playful
MANIA-Passionate   *AGAPE*-Altruism

"When you have learned about love,
you have learned of God."
Fox Indian Proverb

Acts of altruism come in the form of holding the door open for someone, anonymously sending money, contributing energy or money to a local charity, picking up a neighbor's newspaper, pitching in to help someone going through a difficult time because they are unable to function at their normal level, sending a thank-you note, working in a soup kitchen, reading to the elderly or a child, volunteering for a social cause that would improve the lives of many or writing a letter or calling someone just because. The list of altruistic acts can go on into infinity. And they are the very definition of selflessness.

We all need to keep others in our hearts, but there will come several critical times in your life when it is best not to shower your loved ones with all of their desires. At times, love is expressed by standing up for oneself, no longer tolerating an abusive relationship and leaving.

Love is, at times, the ability to withhold. This will come in the form of doing what's best for others by not giving them what they believe they want or need at the time. The result is a form of compassionate caring, tough love, through discipline.

Love is also setting limits and establishing a clear line between wants and needs. The child, or adult, may interpret this as cruel, but in the end it will be seen as a valuable stepping-stone along life's journey.

Love is giving a child the needed reinforcement of empathy as well as guidance.

"In the evening of your life, you will be judged by love."
Saint John of the Cross

"The goal of a human is to love, to live,
to learn and to leave a legacy."
Steven Covey

The results of George Valliant's 40-year Harvard study on personality traits that help to stave off or minimize a midlife crisis revealed some surprising results. Over 200 men were tested and followed-up over the years to discover the traits of wellness. Our assumptions on the factors related to mental and physical health have at times, been misleading. Is it where they live? Whether they had a happy childhood? What types of food they ate, or didn't eat? Happily married? Good profession? The way in which these men navigated through life in a healthy way was to use these five psychological defenses:

Altruism— (**this chapter**) This is the movement away from one's self to the unselfish acts for the welfare of others.

Humor— (**chapter #5**) The coping strategy used to de-escalate a situation. It is the ability to see the comedy within any situation.

Sublimation— (**chapter #8**) Redirecting energy from an unacceptable activity to an acceptable one. The child who is a thrill seeker/hero grows up to be a firefighter.

Anticipation— (chapter #15) The ability to look ahead at problems to find the best solutions before they happen.

Suppression—(**buried everywhere**) The conscious ability to avoid thinking about stressful or unpleasant events.

Another approach to a higher understanding of love of others is the practice of Buddhist meditation:

1. Generosity;
2. Virtue and ethics — speaking and act in ways that do not harm others;
3. Training of the heart and mind.

> *The purpose of prayer and meditation is to come to the realization that you no longer think or feel that you are a part of the whole, but you truly **know** you are a part of the whole.*

In Maslow's characteristics of a self-actualized individual, the attribute of goodness/benevolence is one of the values of Being — an individual's fellowship with humanity.

"I think I began learning long ago that those who are happiest are those who do the most for others."
Booker T. Washington

> In the final analysis, we can reduce these overt unselfish acts to love and compassion. When love is in the forefront, the clarity of the beauty of the world is in clear focus.

If you become a professional volunteer or over-commit yourself to volunteerism, there is a strong likelihood of burnout. If there is more pain than pleasure, then back off of your giving. It will do you and the recipient little benefit if you have overburdened yourself. Altruism doesn't require constant subjugation of your own needs and wants. Take care of yourself!

> *Be mindful of the thought that the opposite of love is not hate, but apathy!*

CHAPTER 5

A Funny Thing Didn't Happen To Me On The Way To My Disorder

Did you know that the National Institute of Mental Health has issued a statement announcing that it will no longer use field rats in its psychological experiments? The board unanimously agreed that it will instead use attorneys, for the following reasons: 1) Since they breed like rabbits, there are more attorneys than rats in our society; 2) they found that the experimenters became less attached to the attorneys than the rats; and 3) there are some things that even a rat wouldn't do.

This whole area of humor has always been of special interest to me. Coming from a family of humorous people, it still amazes me that other people and families take themselves so seriously. In my study of human development, I have come to realize that the absence of laughter can be reduced to one single word — responsibility. We learn to grow out of our wonder and joy that we had as a child. When we mature and gain a greater sense of responsibility in our lives, the intellectual concept of humor becomes obsolete. The two concepts should not, and will not go side by side. Or so we are conditioned to believe.

One of the first qualities that subside as people go through an episode of depression is their sense of humor. This is especially evident in their lack of ability to see the humor they possess within themselves, and to laugh.

The Greek philosopher Democritus, who lived to the age of 100, knew the value of laughter when he emphasized well-being based on cheerfulness and the freedom from worry. Plato and Socrates are associated with one of the earliest theories of laughter. Medical history even indicates that laughter was used as an anesthetic for surgical procedures back in the 13th century, and in the 16th century it was prescribed as treatment for colds and depression. In Medieval times the court jester entered the great dining halls to entertain guests, since laughter was believed to aid in digestion.

Sigmund Freud wrote an entire section on humor and called it the highest of the defensive processes an individual possesses. George Valliant's 40-year prospective study called "Adaptation To Life" could only find 5 ways of effective coping by the healthy participants – and a healthy, mature sense of humor ranked among the highest.

Couples who related the factors significant in the longevity of their marriages cited "having fun together" as extremely important. Studies outlining the psychological characteristics of the people who live to be 100 years of age and above found that most of them possessed an unusual sense of humor. Maslow's studies with self-actualized individuals found that one of the 15 characteristics they all displayed was "a good sense of humor tending to be philosophical and nonhostile in their jokes."

Families that can laugh together in a positive way help children develop good character. This is a normal part of the psychological and physiological development of a growing child. When families laugh together, they create an experiential bond. Through trial and error, they are able to differentiate the good humor from the inappropriate. It is no mystery that the most important ingredient in character development is positive, caring relationships with those whom they live.

One of the reasons we need to have children, or at the very least, be around children, is to remind us of the joy and fun in the world. This is how we are able to reconnect with the lives we used to live when we were free of anxiety and responsibility.

Writer, editor, and statesman Norman Cousins recovered from a degenerative illness, severe ankylosing spondylitis, in which he was given a 1 in 500 chance of surviving. He discovered that if negative emotions can have negative physiological and psychological consequences, then surely positive emotions would have positive effects. Cousins announced that he was taking responsibility for his treatment. Every day he watched Candid Camera and Marx Brothers movies that helped to induce belly laughter (a mini-workout), and as a result was able to sleep without pain medication. He was eventually cured of this disease and went on to write two excellent books on the strong relationship between mind and body.

At the end of his fight, Cousins' doctor said, "The relationship of Mr. Cousins' treatment to his recovery was not clearly understood nor adequately explained, and was initiated at the specific insistence of Mr. Cousins. To date, I have not clearly established a rational cause, nor how Mr. Cousins cured himself via his own hand and mind."

Laughter and humor are psychologically healing and an excellent form of exercise. Dr. William Fry researched the benefits of laughter and found that it increases the heart rate and respiration, decreases blood pressure, improves digestion, works the muscles in the face and stomach, increases beta-endorphines and catecholamines and enhances circulation. When the laughter subsides, the body enters into a relaxed state.

Our mindset can be reduced to two contrasting modes: open and closed. The open mode is more relaxed, receptive, exploratory, playful and humorous. The closed mode (which we find ourselves in most of the time) is tighter, rigid and pressured to be focused. The arts of learning, creativity and healing are more responsive in the open mode of relating to yourself and the world. It's a choice of living we sometimes have to encourage ourselves to make.

Our ability to step back from events and see the humor contained there is valuable in many ways. Of all the health benefits, the most important is its ability to tame and soothe the stressor-rich environment that we live in. Managers and leaders who use humor and demonstrate laughter are seen as approachable, creative, confident, flexible, trustworthy and, most importantly, *human*!

If you make the conscious decision to include humor in your workplace, keep in mind that you will have to confront several misconceptions surrounding this life-promoting act:

1. People will no longer take me seriously if they see me using humor when I communicate. The truth: As I just said, and it bears repeating, managers and leaders are seen as approachable, creative, confident, flexible, trustworthy and, most importantly, more human when they are light-hearted.

2. Humor cannot be in a business that should be taken very seriously. The truth: Every business is serious, isn't it? Take your job seriously, but not yourself.

3. To be humorous, you have to be a born comedian. The truth: This is truly nurture over nature. Children on the average will laugh 200 to 300 times a day, while adults have been reduced to an average of only 17! Do you believe Robin Williams came out of the womb performing? (Well, OK, maybe he did, but he's the only one!)

4. If humor is allowed, employees will be doing it all the time instead of focusing on work. The truth: This is an irrational type of all-or-nothing thinking. Some humor is better than no humor at all. Every healthy workplace has a mixture of laughter within the business.

5. Humor at work may be viewed as inappropriate or offensive. The truth: Sadly, this has become truer in recent years, as the

politically correct thought police patrol the halls at work looking for the slightest indication of a "hostile work environment" (which, of course, begs the question, "hostile in whose opinion?"). It also is another example of all-or-nothing thinking, so just go ahead and throw the baby out with the bathwater! Don't let the thought police win. No matter what a few misguided malcontents say, harmless fun is still harmless fun. Of course you must still be discreet and sensitive. And jokes based upon race, gender, ethnicity and such are inappropriate. But there's still plenty of room for laughter.

6. People don't get humor, so why try? The truth: Most people do. Certainly some individuals have a total lack of humor in their personality; so don't take it too personally when they don't see the value in a mature sense of humor and fun. There are some people who just don't get it and they probably never will. We should have pity on them and pray that they are not in leadership roles.

A focus on health and humor can lead to a long and happy life. Consider the case of the 80 year-old man who went to a doctor for his check-up. The doctor told him, "You are in amazingly great shape. There's nothing wrong with you; you're as strong as an ox and your heart and lungs are like someone in his 30s. I can almost guarantee you a long and healthy life. By the way, if it's not too personal, how old was your father when he died?" The 80-year-old patient responded, "Did I say he was dead?" The doctor couldn't believe it! So he said, "How old was your grandfather when he died?" The 80-year-old again responded, "Did I say he was dead?" The doctor was astonished! He said, "You mean to tell me you're 80 years old and both your father and grandfather are still alive?" "Not only that," said the patient, "my grandfather is 126 years old, and next week he's getting married!" The doctor said, "At 126 years of age, why on Earth did your grandfather want to get married?" His patient looked up at the doctor and said, "Did I say he *wanted* to?"

Humor is simply a shift of perspective. It is nothing more and nothing less. It is the ability to reframe a situation and find the joy and humor that resides within it.

"Laughter is the sound of freedom."
Sheldon Kopp

"Do not take life too seriously.
You will never get out of it alive."
Elbert Hubbard

So, an honest lawyer walks into a bar and the bartender looks up and says, "Hey what is this, a joke?"

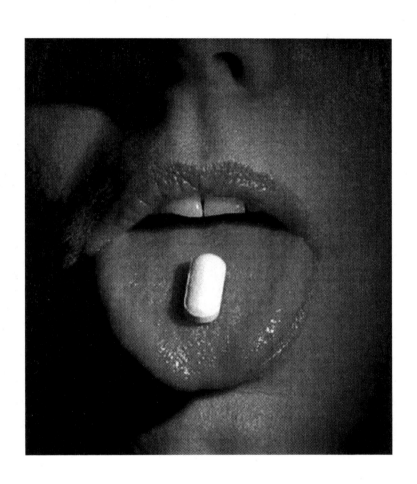

CHAPTER 6

Belief is the placebo that leads to success

"There are mysteries, above all the mystery of the relationship of mind and body, that will never be explained, not by the most brilliant doctors, the wisest of scientists or philosophers."
Stewart Alsop

"You are the result of everything that you have thought."
Buddha

What is the common thread that is woven through these people?

1). Melissa consults her physician because of a cold she can't shake. Antibiotics won't help because her condition has been determined to be viral. She believes the cold could be turning into pneumonia and requests antibiotics. The doctor writes her a prescription for a strong antibiotic, but it is actually a simple sugar pill. Once she starts taking the pill, the cold disappears.

2). Ryan has had a persistent and pounding headache prior to taking his exams throughout his school years. He has come to rely heavily on over-the-counter headache medication to relieve his pain. During his high school years, his parents decide to start giving him Vitamin C tablets, which closely resemble the shape of his prior medication. Within 15 minutes, his headache subsides.

3). Anna develops cancer and goes through the standard surgery and chemotherapy treatments. Believing in the strong healing power of the mind, she practices meditation, biofeedback, creates optimism, forgives all of his enemies, begins to truly love everyone deeply and stops blaming herself for contracting the disease. Not only does she begin to feel better, she also remains in remission for several years.

4). Lloyd has had persistent arthritis for years and has gone through all types of medication protocols. At a weekend healing retreat, he is introduced to the magical healing power of a copper pyramid. With the support of his group and an upbeat approach to this type of treatment, he no longer experiences the persistent pain that had hindered him for years.

5). A power lifter has hit an impasse. She has been stuck on the same amount of bench press weight for over six months and her coach attempts a new approach to her training. For her final lift, the coach secretly places an additional 10 pounds on the bar. She approaches the bench, goes through her routine, lifts and benches the weight with the same ease that she had several minutes prior to the change.

A group of Harvard researchers wanted to test people in a clinic. Now of course, the people in the study felt much better after they had gone to the clinic and seen the doctor. With more questioning, they found that the people *in* the waiting room as well as people who had just made an appointment began to feel better too. Everybody wins! What these people have in common is belief. It is the mysterious phenomenon of the mind working in tandem with the body to enhance healing: the placebo response, which in Latin means, "I shall be pleasing." They are the benefits that are derived from the mere suggestion of effectiveness.

It occurs when we receive certain types of messages from the environment. These messages work at some level to alter the meaning of our state of health or illness. These messages activate the inner apothecary of our minds.

Historically, medicine first discovered the effect of this "symbolic significance" on health by seeing improvement in patients who were given bread, sugar pills or other dummy medicines that could exert only a symbolic power.

This placebo effect is a mysterious combination of the mind working in tandem with the physiology to increase the healing process. These messages somehow stimulate our inner apothecary in a way that can only be explained by a strong belief system.

One hundred first-year medical students were once divided into two groups for a double blind experiment on the power of suggestion. The researcher presenting the super-stimulant and the super-tranquilizers did not know the contents of each pill. The researcher for the first group presented the students with what he called a "Super-stimulant" for them to consume. Prior to the ingestion of the red pill, he explained to them the effects as well as the side effects. After taking the pill, over half of the students experienced exactly what was suggested to them.

In the second group, the researcher presented them with a "Super-tranquilizer" which was colored blue. He again told them of the potential effects and side effects. The pill was then taken and over half of these students experienced what was suggested to them.

At the end of this study, what was most striking was not the fact that the majority of the participants did what was suggested, but something even more dramatic. The contents of the pills were switched. That's right, the super-stimulant in the red pill was actually replaced with the super-tranquilizer, and vice versa.

What this meant was that the students had to work even harder (mentally and physically) to fulfill the suggested effects of the researcher. It would have been accepted, placebo wise, if the contents were neutral, but they were actually pushing beyond what their body was actually doing. Thus, the power of suggestion created a kind of mind-over-matter reality for the participants.

In another classic experiment, elementary school teachers were notified that each of their classrooms contained all gifted children or all slow learners. This has been replicated several times with nearly identical results. At the beginning of the school year, the teachers walked into their respective classrooms with the expectation that they were addressing the brightest or the most difficult. At the end of the year, you guessed it; the brightest became the best and the slow learners lived up to their teacher's expectations. This is the self-fulfilling prophecy at work, with both placebo and nocebo — the negative benefits derived from attaching a negative meaning to the treatment (or to life).

Many years ago, a patient had cancer with tumors throughout his lymph system. A miracle cure was announced for his type of cancer, so the doctor ordered the medication. The cure worked because his tumors shrank. The newspapers caught wind of this new treatment and found that it was not as effective as was earlier reported. He became very discouraged and his tumors began to grow again.

The medical team, knowing that the power of suggestion had been partially responsible for his reaction to the medication, decided to tell him that a more powerful batch had just been released. Using only sterile water injections, he began to show incredible improvements.

His remission lasted until the newspaper, once again, showed that his medication was worthless. His tumors grew and shortly thereafter, he died.

SUGGESTIONS IN = RESULTS OUT

Many years ago in a Los Angeles football stadium, a half dozen people reported falling ill with severe poisoning. The physician upon close examination ascertained that they had all consumed soda from under the stands. In an attempt to protect others, he ordered an announcement be made, requesting that no one have soft drinks from the dispensing machines from under the stands. With that stadium announcement, the entire stadium began to become sick. Emergency rooms in five county hospitals were filled, people consulted their own physicians and over 200 people had to be hospitalized.

Later the word was passed along that the incident was coincidental and not the ill effects of the soda dispensers. As quickly as they became ill, they became well.

The point of these vignettes is that we can become ill or sick as a result of how we think. As Virgil Aeneid said in 19 B.C., "They can because they think they can." There appears to be a consistent thread of "mind-over-matter" in the body's ability to move into a healing phase because the mind expects it to take place.

This mind-over-matter effectiveness is threefold:
The belief of the healer.
The belief of the recipient.
The belief in the special relationship that exists between the two.

Thoughts, feelings or self-destructive internal dialogue do not cause disorders. However, your frame of mind can, studies show, put you at a significant advantage or disadvantage. To a certain degree, all the different aspects of an individual, mind and body, interact with, and influence, one another.

Let me also emphasize the common misinterpretation of some of these *thoughts=illness or health* dialogues. Let's be real, and not become fanatical with the will of the mind over other types of approaches to overall health and wellness. If I were to encounter a serious condition, not only would I direct my thoughts and actions toward a more optimistic perspective, but I would also grab the best type of medical intervention available. The two working in tandem is much better, by far, than relying solely on one's own self-healing suggestive abilities.

Whether it is a personal and/or business goal that you are attempting to reach, keep this in mind:

> **"Whether you believe you can,**
> **or believe you can't, you're right."**
> **Henry Ford**

CHAPTER 7

I drink, therefore I relax....
Yeah, right!

"Many have fallen with the bottle in their hand."
Lakota Indian Proverb

Relaxation is the art of quieting the mind and calming the body.

Biofeedback, music, guided imagery, reverie, Judeo-Christian prayer, transcendental meditation, mantras, yoga, Zen, Tai Chi, breath counting, progressive muscular relaxation, autogenic training, warm baths, fly fishing, golf, gardening, calming aphorisms, etc. — there must over a thousand different ways to reach a relaxed state in an acceptable manner. There are as many ways to achieve this tranquil state of mind, as there are different personalities. The true secret is finding the right one for you at this particular time in your life.

In reality, the method by which a relaxed state is reached is inconsequential – as long as it doesn't involve illegal drugs, excessive alcohol or any television programs involving a slimy sensation seeking talk show host. Masturbation also will make you go blind. What becomes important, rather, is if you do it, and how often you do it.

There continues to be an ongoing debate about whether it is more beneficial to sit quietly for an extended period of time or to take several mini-relaxation breaks throughout the day. I'm not sure why there is so much discussion over this, because any time devoted to the act is much better than no time at all. Some people cannot find the time to sit in reverie for a half hour or more, so they need to choose the mini-breaks.

Relaxation parallels exercise in that allotting time to these practices is the key to experiencing the benefits of each.

The goal of any form of relaxation is to quiet the mind and calm the body. If you are feeling better, physically and mentally at the end of the technique, then you are doing it right. Plain and simple, is it not?

Of the thousands of possibilities to achieve a relaxed and calm state, the easiest way is the most destructive way. The reason so many mind-altering drugs have risen to epidemic proportions is that the resulting high is achieved with the least amount of effort in the quickest possible time.

The truth is, any significant and meaningful transformation in your state of mind will take time and discipline to get there. But we live in a quick fix, lightening-speed society, so the fastest road to get there is the best. The ads for the 8 minutes to Zen mastery are very appealing for our culture of Type A personalities. We want it fast and we demand it now!

As part of our cultural belief system, it is not looked upon as being productive if you are sitting, simply doing nothing. In reality, the short- and long-term benefits of relaxation are overwhelming:

➤ Reduction in blood pressure
➤ Clarity of thoughts
➤ Increased blood circulation throughout the body
➤ Overall stress and anxiety reduction
➤ Greater body awareness
➤ A lessening of psychosomatic disorders (i.e., headaches)

Instant relaxation is an oxymoron, because achieving the state of true relaxation takes time, patience, discipline and persistence.

So in enters Bob. Bob came to the hospital to be evaluated because his parents believed he had a serious problem. Bob's parents had to escort him to the hospital because he did not feel that he had a problem. Bob was 42 at the time and still living with the folks. His parents said he drank too much. Bob did not perceive a problem because he had never missed a day of work. Therefore, to him the problem was not a problem, just a parental concern.

Bob drank a little.

Bob drank Everclear. (Not to be confused with the musical group)

Everclear is 190 proof grain alcohol.

Bob had 2 pints a day, beginning in the morning, during his breaks and until he blacked out in the evening.

Did Bob have a problem?

This was the only way he could adequately relax.

Bob was a rational and intelligent man who had convinced himself that this was the only way to reach and calm and peaceful state.

If Bob couldn't drink, his mind and body would find a way to get the spirits to make him feel better.

Bob was an alcoholic.

Bob was a serious alcoholic.

Bob was in serious mental and physical trouble.

Bob had to drink to feel good?

Bob didn't know the truth.

Bob was in deep denial.

Bob really needed immediate help.

Bob did get better but he was hesitant.

Bob's parents, who had been aware of his problem for a long time, were also going to be a part of the solution for Bob. The reality is that it is a family problem, not just an individual concern. Because the parents were a part of Bob's world of addiction, they had become enablers of his drinking.

I did not say that they caused it, unless you are of the school that all psychological issues begin with mommy and daddy. But they are now intertwined with the success or failure of his future. That means beginning now!

> Denial of reality is both a wonderful and a disastrous defense mechanism that we rely on to maintain our "normal" state of awareness.

Let me make one point perfectly clear: It is very easy to become addicted — to anything. For some unknown reason, it satisfies a deeper need that we cannot reach at a conscious level. So here we are, a prosperous nation of addicts. Remember that some addictions are socially acceptable, while others haven't received the seal of disapproval yet.

Back when experimenters would conduct tests on living creatures other than humans, they did a little number on a frog. The idea was to draw an analogy between human behavior through other living entities.

The process went like this: The scientists placed a frog into a large container of water at room temperature. Over a very extended period of time, they increased the heat of the water. The little froggie slowly adapted to the changing environment until the water had reached a very high reading.

Even though it was hot, the change was made at such a gradual rate that the frog survived. If the froggie would have been plopped into the heated environment initially, the change in temperature would have had immediate ill effects on it.

This is habituating over time to gradual changes in the environment. The change takes place over an extended period of time.

So, can the same be said about human behavior and thoughts?

One of the most difficult tasks in achieving a relaxed state is the quieting of the mind's constant internal chatter. Those who have taken up different forms of relaxation have reported that they were significantly less depressed, less anxious, angry, confused and distracted than those who remained un-relaxed.

The self-reflection achieved from relaxation brings about a higher state of self-appreciation as well. They also report they felt charged with more energy and less heart and gastrointestinal problems, and that their overall health levels were higher. It also has the ability to reverse the effects of heart disease!

The achievement of a relaxed state can be reached by basically one of two approaches. The goal of Eastern meditation is to reduce the ego until you are without the constraints of your conscious limitations. This road is more time-consuming and the results come slowly. The main idea is to detach the ego connection to the self so that a greater, larger force can be experienced. There is also a lot more humility when the ego has become released in the process.

The goal of Western meditation is to enhance and improve the ego and its functions. Because we are an ego-driven society, our desire is to refine the outward appearance so that the appearance is that of serenity. From this, an admiration is achieved, thus strengthening the ego.

One quick and medically sanctioned application is an abundance of anti-anxiety pills. The relaxed state is achieved at a greatly reduced rate of time. A lot of positive support for this method will come from peers, the American Medical Society, pharmaceutical companies and even insurance companies.

When choosing the best method of relaxation for yourself, one needs to be mindful of the fact that there is no one right way to get to that state of equaniminity. Many people and companies that need to reinforce their way as the correct way will make an attempt, just as the exercise fad folks will, to sensationalize their new state-of-the-art method.

The truth is that there are as many ways to get there, as there are people on the planet. The end result is the achievement of a quiet mind, a calm body and the pleasant experience of *it* while you are engaged in the routine.

CHAPTER 8

IN PURSUIT OF WORK MOTIVATION

OR

Elvis was the King because he found his professional bliss

It was Thomas Carlyle who said, "Blessed is he who has found his work; let him ask no other blessedness." The more people I meet, the more I find that most people don't enjoy what they are doing 40 to 60 hours a week. And why not? Just how are people supposed to feel when they are thrown into a work environment in which they are stripped of their individuality and creativity? When an employer exiles everything uplifting about the human experience, what can you expect except unthinking, unfeeling automatons?

And what a tragedy! People begin work with excitement and anticipation for the future, only to be squashed by the "work protocol" —both the written, as well as the unwritten, rules for performance and behavior. Rules that often are dictatorial, poorly thought-out and overly oppressive.

People who have internal conflict in their work environment have reached the oldest profession of prostitution. They have come to realize that they are selling themselves out at work for the sake of the benefits (money and other rewards). Internally they are struggling with the dilemma of staying and being miserable. They have essentially sold themselves to the company store. Employees end up working in a state of anxiety and depression so that they can live up to a self-determined level of comfort — survival at whatever level of lifestyle they feel they need to live up to. They become hopeless because they are stuck! No wonder there are so many sick workers in our society.

Humans are naturally self-propelled, naturally motivated organisms, but what actually motivates individuals can be so unclear. We have plenty in common, but so much that makes us unique. Most work places, most work protocols, don't take our humanity into consideration, much less our individuality!

> **NEED>DRIVE>RESPONSE>ATTAINMENT OF THE GOAL>SATISFACTION OF THE NEED**

The meaning of work has changed throughout time, depending on the societal conditions and economic factors. The three basic meanings regarding work are: (1) Work is necessary, painful and burdensome, (2) work is a means toward an end and (3) work is a creative act that is good for its own sake.

Why are we all so burned up, burned out and depressed? Well, gee, maybe it's because any of us would be miserable working in a job for over 40 hours a week that rewards us with little or no personal satisfaction! Something has gone wrong in our working lives, and here are some leading symptoms of that:

- The greatest percentage of heart attacks takes place on Monday mornings (black Monday).

- We will work one month longer than in 1970 and two months longer than Europeans.
- Workers' compensation claims related to stress have tripled.
- Our youth are working so much it is interfering with their class activities.
- People are sleeping less than what is recommended for optimal health. Either because of overwhelming thoughts or limited time pressures.
- Companies are looking for people who are always there or who can be contacted immediately through telephones, cell phones, beepers, faxes and e-mails; no matter where you are, you are in constant contact with work. They would prefer you sleep there too.
- More is demanded from fewer people with less time and many times with fewer resources.
- Most of the country believes that they have little time for their families.
- Our free time has fallen dramatically. When we have free time we often feel guilty about not producing business related results.
- Children are left at home while the parents are at work – meaning less adult guidance, more unwanted pregnancies and lost youth, and more power for the slim talk show hosts of the world.

Job satisfaction comes from a good fit between work and a person's interests, abilities, needs, and expectations. In the 1970s workers rated "interesting work" as the most important aspect of work. A second survey in the 1980s found that "satisfying and rewarding work" ranked first in preference.

The mix for a perfect fit in a job is simple, and here it is:

The intersection of your interests with your abilities will create your strengths. When you are able to focus in on your true strengths, you will find the perfect fit, not only for the organization, but also for you! Don't just find a job, find your strength and all will prosper.

Your interests are those activities that motivate you. You may be interested in an endless string of activities, from gardening to engineering. The intent, or interest is here, but you lack the requisite framework to do it. Or, you may have the framework, but are unable to accomplish the end results.

Your abilities are your true talents. Do you find it to be extremely easy to communicate, create, manage people, analyze, and/or synthesize?

The greatest concerns for employers are: (1) finding good employees; (2) strategic planning; (3) maintaining a high performance climate; (4) improving customer satisfaction and (5) reducing stress.

Leaders, managers and supervisors are all struggling with the concerns listed above. They also need to be aware of what the employees are looking for in their form of management.

A study conducted in the late 1990s revealed that the most important employee motivation came from: (1) appreciation; (2) being "in" on things; (3) sympathy for personal problems; (4) job security; (5) wages; (6) interesting work; (7) promotions; (8) employer's loyalty; (9) working conditions and (10) tactful discipline.

To summarize the research conducted in this area, job satisfaction is highest when workers are (1) allowed ordinary social contacts with others; (2) given opportunities to use their own judgment and intelligence; (3) recognized for doing well; (4) given a chance to apply their skills; (5) given relative freedom from close supervision and (6) given opportunities for promotion and advancement.

Where does your internal drive and motivation come from?

Extrinsic (external) motivation comes from obvious external rewards such as pay, company benefits, grades, rewards and/or approval. Extrinsic motivators are more important for dissatisfaction.

Intrinsic (internal) motivation occurs when there appears to be no obvious external reward. The activity one is engaged in is an end in itself. This is what Maslow spoke of when he viewed higher-level growth needs. These are the needs that truly fulfill our human potential. Intrinsic motivators are more important for satisfaction.

Before any type of motivational or attitudinal climate can change, management and leaders must take a closer look at the three types of environments their people are working under. These three are important for many reasons; the main two are that there is a strong and direct correlation between certain types of management/leadership styles and the amount of depression experienced, apathy felt and sick time used.

What I am attempting to illuminate here is that you must focus in on the cultural climate of an organization before you marry into it! I f you marry into the wrong relationship, then you have just stepped into a potentially abusive environment!

> **Theory X- KITA (Old business approach, Kick'em In The…)** Motivation comes through the pay, fringe benefits, and the security of having a job. This could be called the external rewards for simply doing the job. In this type of old business world environment, the emphasis is placed on punishment, and management has the overruling power in all decisions. Workers toil in a state of helplessness, with very little responsibility beyond the function of their job.

> **Theory Y- (Changed as the work force changed)** Here, more motivation comes from an employee's valued input. There is a strong emphasis on rewards and trust, and more responsibility is granted workers, including more control over their working conditions. With more control comes greater internal contentment and greater satisfaction. This begins to move into intrinsic satisfaction over one's performance.

> ➢ **Theory Z- (The whole becomes greater than the sum of its parts)** Drawn from Japanese culture and business, this model features complete worker participation in creating their surroundings. All levels work together to create a consensus on business decisions. Not only does this improve human relations, it also strengthens the internal power of the participant, and the worker's commitment to the success of the organization.

The truth of the matter is that the old forms of management no longer work. We are operating in a fast paced, constantly changing work environment and the old methods are too rigid and prone to internal destruction. Our work relationships are extremely important to our overall health. If you consider how much time you spend in the work environment, you may as well consider it your second family. You spend more waking moments within the workspace than you do with your actual family. So, my question is, how healthy is your family? Keep in mind that no family is completely functional. A functional family is truly an oxymoron!

Job enrichment, empowerment, teamwork or terms similar to these, are the new buzz phrases which involves removing some of the controls and restrictions on employees, giving them greater responsibility, freedom, choice, and authority. Whenever possible, workers are given feedback about their work or progress. This feedback comes to them directly, instead of to a supervisor. Workers are encouraged to learn new and more difficult tasks and to learn a broad range of skills. This lowers production costs, increases job satisfaction, improves workers' attitudes, reduces boredom, and less absenteeism.

Freud's simplistic explanation of true happiness consisted of only two endeavors: work and love.

Top Reasons To Stay At A Job (in order)

Career growth, exciting work and challenge, meaningful work and making a difference or contribution, great people to work with, being part of a team, good boss, recognition for a job well-done, autonomy or a sense of control over work, flexible work hours and dress code.

The three main reasons people are experiencing higher levels of stress in the workplace (and life) can be reduced to:

1). The volatile dynamics of people's personalities and their positions within a hierarchy can create friction.
2). Overflow of information (rules, regulations, changing agendas, etc...)
3). The ever-changing world of technology (more complicated and faster)

Theodore Roosevelt said, "Far and away the best prize that life offers is the chance to work hard at work worth doing." Of the thousands of possible careers people can choose from, then why is it that the majority of first time heart attacks occur on Monday mornings between 8 and 9 a.m.? People are experiencing misery as they enter the Monday work environment.

We all must learn to find the special reasons for being, relating, and creating in this world. It is possible to get your uniqueness from your profession. The main reasons why individuals refuse to follow their *bliss* can be for one or all of the following reasons:

1) If I find what it is, it will be completely unacceptable.
2) If I find it, there will no room in this world to do it.
3) If I find it, it will have such contradictory elements, I will not be able to do it.
4) I just may get everything that I've ever wanted (and that's scary)!

There are many ways to get *it* from your profession.

One way could be to simply quit your job, especially if it causes you great distress. On the average, we will go through 3 to 10 major career changes in our lifetime. Is the time for you to change now?

Another possibility is to get support from your employer to advance your skills through work-related training. The last option you have is to stay, submit yourself to the internal pain, and model the lifestyle of a martyr.

Whatever it will take to find your perfect fit, from reading books, taking career courses, getting a coach or mentor, or simply start doing what you love doing, then get started now!

Ashley Montague summarized overall health as the ability to work, the ability to love, the ability to laugh and play, and the ability to use one's mind.

"If a man is called to be a street sweeper, he should sweep streets even
as Michelangelo painted, or Beethoven composed music, or
Shakespeare wrote poetry. He should sweep streets so well that all the
hosts of Heaven and Earth will pause to say, here lived a great street
sweeper who did his job well."
The Reverend Martin Luther King Jr.

(If all else fails, listen and sing along with Elvis)

CHAPTER 9

Dr. Laura is not a psychologist, Rush Limbaugh becomes even more redundant and the IRS is very difficult to work with

(How listening to some people can make you sick. Nothing personal to Dr. Laura and Rush, however, very personal to the IRS)

**"The last of our human freedoms is to choose
our attitude in any circumstance."
Victor Frankl**

You will be judged by those you choose to associate with. Not only will you be judged, but you will also adapt and adopt their thought processes. Peoples' attitudes and behaviors are extremely contagious, and if you listen long enough you will develop the same mindset and thought process.

It becomes a familiar rite-of-passage dialogue that takes place between parents and their growing children: "Why are you hanging out with those kinds of friends? Don't you realize that you are going to be judged by the company you keep? The good, the bad, and the toxic!"

"Those who lie down with the dogs get up with fleas."
Blackfoot Indian Proverb

There are many toxic people in this world! Those who drain you and those who will shame you. These are the naysayers: The day will never be sunny and no one around me should be allowed to enjoy their lives (because mine is so miserable, so let me tell you about it).

I mentioned Dr. Laura, Rush Limbaugh and the IRS in my chapter heading because all three have a large following. Of course, the IRS has the dubious distinction of having by far the largest following, with statistically the smallest amount of loyal supporters.

The Dr. and The Rush have a plethora of followers, even though the fine Laura received her Ph.D. in physiology, not psychology, but has the ability to dole out mental health advice rather that what she is educated in. Maybe her real world experiences prior to her mental health training gives her the expertise to dispense moral advice? Folks, it's nothing but speaking to the listeners who need to be reprimanded! We have all sinned, her philosophy goes, and the Dr. of physiology will remind us of our shortcomings and wail away, preaching "The World According to Dr. Laura." If people really needed this type of abuse, they could stay stuck in whatever mode they were in prior to the beating the Dr. of physiology would give.

And then there are the fine, ditto-headed followers of Rush Limbaugh. He is the king of berating certain types of people and their personal views. His claim to fame is that whether you were listening to him many years ago, or yesterday, his song is exactly the same. Oh sure, he has a few more trite stories to tell, but they have the same theme and outcome. If there is a strong desire within you to expand yourself, create your own ideas, which are actually stimulating, then you need to delete his modulation from your radio and listen to silence.

Then, there is the customer-friendly IRS agent. Such a large and powerful organization in which the paying customer is always wrong and is placed in a defensive position unless they can prove their innocence. Now, wait a minute here; we as citizens of the United States need to consider it an honor to live in such a wonderful country. Part of the reason we have such opportunity and freedom is through the tax system, which I completely agree with. So, let me make that point crystal clear!

A close encounter with a real IRS agent (Undercover)!

I came to the realization that some people have great difficulty making change (metaphorically) when I was taking a limo ride in a large eastern city. I was having a lively discussion with a dentist about his practice and researching why they have such a highly stressful profession. I believe it was the only time I had ever spoken to a dentist without sharp scraping devices being used on my teeth. After he was dropped off at his destination, the driver spoke up.

He said, "You know I was listening to you men talk about stress and disorders and I have a couple of comments. First of all, I'm not really a limo driver. (I thought, oh my God, what's coming next?) This is not my full time job. You see, I only do this to relax and meet friendly people. My daytime job creates a lot of stress in my life because of the angry people I have to deal with."

So I thought maybe he was a parole officer or postal worker.

"I am an IRS agent"

I knew they existed because I have spoken to pretty much every one of them, but I had never actually met one. It was my belief that they all kept undercover and used another profession when someone asked them what they did for a living!

So I asked a leading question: "I understand you all have placed a greater emphasis on customer service lately, so how is that working?"

He became very angry (surprise!) and went into a long explanation about how the IRS does not have to be customer friendly. "These people owe us money and they should just pay it. I have heard so many excuses why they cannot pay what they owe. That's what causes me so much stress."

It was a long ride and I changed the subject to sports so he had some time to cool down.

We exchanged farewells as he was handing me the receipt for the $20 ride. He let me know that the IRS would allow a $70 deduction for this ride even though it was only $20. "Wouldn't that be cheating if I filled it out for more that it actually was?" "Well officially, not really because that's what they allow."

I gave him a $2 tip and claimed $22 on my taxes. I am sure the agents will find that deduction when they audit me. I guess IRS agents are people too. People just like us!

When you have been given the unpleasant opportunity to carry on a mature, adult-like conversation with these folks, you can quickly be reduced to a pseudo-criminal who is trying to take advantage of their uncomplicated tax laws. That is, after you have hit the dial tone buttons on your phone approximately 127 times.

When I have shared my own IRS nightmares with others, which is a type of emotional support, I have learned that I was not alone. As a matter of fact, everyone that I spoke to confirmed my finding. After their IRS histories were shared, I felt so much better. I guess there is some value in sharing emotionally jarring experiences.

Now, I am certain I am setting myself up for more conversations with the agents. I will make a promise to you secret agent man/woman: Work with me and I will work with you. Talk to me as if I am a law-abiding, tax-paying proud American, and I will do the same for you.

Thank you, and the check is once again, in the mail. If not, you can call my toll free number and stay on the line for about 30 minutes. I'm sorry, but we are a little short staffed around here; we're out working!

The point here is that negative gravity is all around you to drag you down as far as you will let it. They'll bash you directly, fill your head with subtle negativity and paranoia – or, as in the aggravated case of the IRS, treat you like a criminal.

The imprinted messages that we are constantly receiving come from a multitude of sources: TV, radio, music, printed materials, computers, social contacts, dreams and solitude, as well as the memories that continue to float back into our consciousness. And they all have their own gravitational pull.

Parents who are aware of their kids' friends know the influence they will have on a developing character. Occasionally, parents will have to have a heart-to-heart talk with their child (especially an adolescent) about the type of people they are hanging around with.

When you associate with people, over time, you be will almost hypnotically seduced to their mindset and begin to believe that this is the way the world should be viewed.

If you want to learn a new activity, whom would you gravitate toward? If you sincerely want to work though a troubling issue, whom would you seek out? If you want to become more informed about a growth-enhancing endeavor, where do you go? Whom do high achievers surround themselves with? We will generate our life energy by moments of solitude as well as the life force that is offered to us by others.

The reality is that we are drawn to the type of people we need to learn something from. Whether we are aware of it or not, we associate with the people who will teach us an important lesson we have not learned from a prior teacher! Whether we make a conscious or unconscious choice, we will gravitate toward these individuals for further lessons. We might not even approve of the lessons they are delivering, but this class is essential for our growth and development!

The influence of others is highlighted in this example: Psychiatrist James Anthony believed that the best way to understand the causes of mental illness is to study the offspring of mentally ill parents. He looked at 300 children of schizophrenics and followed them for 12 years. Most of them did develop mental illness, but surprisingly, 10 percent of the children were unusually well-adapted.

The findings revealed several important relevant factors. First, the less emotionally involved a child is with a sick parent, the less likely the child is to have emotional problems. It was the unusual capacity for these children to detach from the sick parent or sick environment and the ability to recruit a "good enough" relationship with a healthy adult that saved them from "inheriting" mental illness. They developed good social skills and a strong desire to help others. They had hobbies and creative interests that were nurturing and provided meaning. And like stress-resilient adults, these children seemed to have faith that things will work out as well as can reasonably be expected.

That study brings us back to an important and disputed point: Even though outside influences may be negative and counter to growth enhancement, individuals are able to rise above the negativity and prosper. Most of us are capable of saving ourselves in this way – but don't. The majority of us allow ourselves to be pulled down into the underworld of lifelong negativity.

I thoroughly believe the strength lies within us to take in the outside environmental stimuli and interpret it in a way that makes a lot of sense, and is fully grounded in reality, and yet does minimal harm to our sense of well-being and our optimism.

There are fundamentally three types of group energy:
The Optimists—situations are always brighter than they appear
The Pessimists—situations will always be viewed as hopeless
The Steady Neutralists—not the type to overreact or under react, just take it as is.

The contagious influence of others is like falling into a deep hypnotic trance, but in this case it is much larger. We can call it a cultural trance in which the opinions of others infiltrate into our psyches.

We all have varying levels of suggestibility to outside stimuli. With repeated suggestions given to a receptive audience, there is a great probability that these messages will become fact. These master hypnotists (talk show gurus) administer thoughts, attitudes, beliefs and self-imposed facts onto the listeners with the hope that they can convince them of "THEIR WAY". Once "THEIR WAY" connects with the participants, many of them begin to truly believe the new view of the world, which affects their critical mode of thinking.

This merges into the areas of persuasion, conformity, and attitude change. The area subsumed under the term "hypnotism" is a social psychological phenomenon *par excellence* in that one individual exerts a potential influence on the behavior and experience of another individual.

Now is a good time to mention my three favorite professions: dentists, psychiatrists and funeral directors. Assertions about which occupational group have the most suicides have been floating around like urban myths for decades. It has been stated, quite defensively, that the statistics are difficult to gather. According to the experts within these professions, there is little reliable data available that verifies this alleged risk. They continue to repeat that the relationship between professional stress and suicide has not been substantiated or quantified.

Each work environment presents its own set of stressors, but from conversations with these three groups, they seem to take the prize.

Look at what they have in common:

#1—-No one has a strong desire to see these professions.

#2—-Fear and anxiety are projected onto these people.

#3—-Physical and psychological pain of self and others is hard to
        deal with.

#4—-If their normal defenses mechanisms aren't strong enough, over time, these projected feelings will erode their personality.

#5—-Some things cannot be cured or fixed.

#6—-They have easy access to drugs.

Thus, while we all have stressors at work, some professions have unique difficulties that challenge the members' ability to pull away from the gravitational pull of negativity and self-destructiveness.

The fact that there are plenty of upstanding examples of all these professions indicates quite clearly, though, that it can be done, and done well – using Frankl's "final freedom": the freedom to choose our own attitude in any circumstance we find ourselves in.

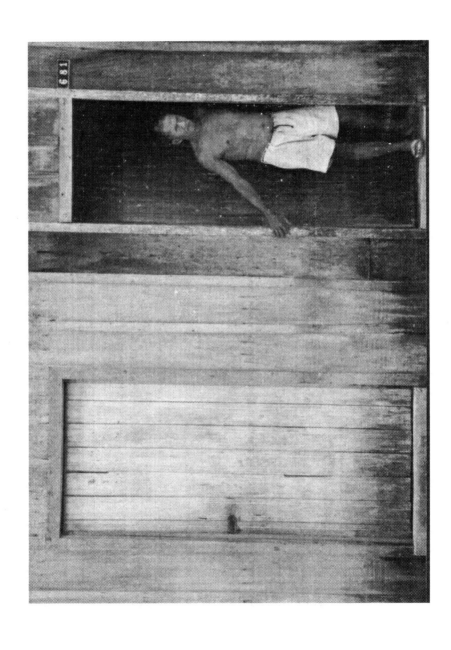

CHAPTER 10

Daring to be different could cause an anxiety attack.

When the Chinese write the word "CRISIS," *they do so with two characters, one meaning* **danger,** *the other meaning* **opportunity.**

"Character cannot be developed in ease and quiet.
Only through experience of trial and suffering can
the soul be strengthened, vision cleared, ambition
inspired and success achieved.
Silver is purified in fire and so are we.
It is in the most trying times
that our real character is shaped and revealed."
Helen Keller

Question: How do you avoid a crisis?
Answer: You can't! However, it now becomes your responsibility to
intelligently and emotionally deal with it.

"There is no warning for upcoming danger."
Cheyenne Indian Proverb

Two roads diverged in a wood, and I—
I took the one less traveled by,
And that has made all the difference.
Robert Frost—-The Road Less Traveled

"Reasonable people adapt themselves to the world.
Unreasonable people attempt to
adapt the world to themselves.
All progress, therefore, depends on unreasonable people."
George Bernard Shaw

It has been said that in life, you will be given a series of God ordained opportunities, brilliantly disguised as crises. No one truly looks forward to having a crisis. But, if you have lived long enough, you realize that they are a part of life and recurring. It's not that you have a crisis or tragedy; it is how you will deal with it that is most important.

Life becomes dull and complacent without an altering experience once in a while. We need to be positioned in a way that we anticipate and move with the never-ending changes that life offers us. We do have one of four reactions to a good crisis; deny it, adapt to it, suppress our natural reactions, or run from it — but you can't run too far or too fast. Eventually, all your inner psychic unresolved issues will present themselves again. We do have choices that we will act upon.

As mentioned earlier, the personality theorist Erik Erikson said that we all face specific psychosocial dilemmas, or "crises" throughout our stages of human development. As we resolve each conflict, we are able to create a new balance between the self and the world. If we have an unfavorable outcome from the "crisis," it will make it more difficult for us to move on to the next. The possibility is that we will continually face this type of crisis later. Those who experience a series of unfavorable outcomes could suffer through a more difficult-than-necessary life challenges.

From interview and questionnaire responses, Gail Sheehy found the "Ten Hallmarks of Well-Being":

1. Life has meaning and direction.
2. **Important transitions in the adult years have been handled in an unusual, personal, or creative way (could these have been opportunities?)**
3. Life has not been disappointing.
4. Long-term goals have already been attained.
5. There is satisfaction with personal growth and development.
6. In love with partner.
7. Many friends.
8. Cheerful person.
9. Not thin-skinned or sensitive to criticism.
10. No major fears.

With the shake-up of a complacent existence, we experience a breakthrough after we move through denial and the shock of it all.

In Eastern traditions, it is understood, even embraced, that enlightenment comes through suffering. It is their belief that there are no accidents in an individual's life and everything that they are going through is in some way necessary for them to move ahead to the next step. There is meaning behind the crisis even if they cannot determine the meaning at that moment. Individuals who have gone through many of these breakthroughs have discovered that "The more difficult the obstacle, the stronger one becomes after hurdling it!"

Many times the overall significance of the meaning behind the misfortune will come to them later.

Any type of major life change, such as death of a loved one, separation, moving, being downsized, physical or mental adjustments can be perceived, in a healthy way, as an individual's *awakening* moment — an awakening because you have just been reminded that life is in a constant state of disharmony and the amount of control you exert over its power is minimal. Now you have an opportunity to react to the change!

This can be seen in every type of cultural or organization change that groups maneuver through. Living with complacency for an extended period of time, every change in a structure will bring about a crisis through a breakthrough in the status quo. During the initial stages prior to the crisis, there is a shock and denial experienced by all who are attempting to make the change. After the change is put into place, there is greater understanding of why it took place and the individual will "buy in" to the new way of thinking. Then the cycle repeats itself, again and again: complacency, crisis and, again, opportunity.

Complacency=shock and denial
Crisis=breakthrough
Opportunity=buy in and adaptation

The ability to handle the disappointments in life is one our greatest challenges, but it becomes the building block of our character development. This type of character development does not end in childhood; it continues throughout our lives. Some people believe they have enough of this type of character development, but I assure you it will never end. We just get better at handling the ups and downs — primarily the downs — of the long journey of our lives.

A crisis will force us to break out of our normal reality, forcing us to create a different reality. The crisis could be that you begin to realize the value of time, or the preciousness of time.

A healthy response to a crisis, after the emotional expressions have been worked through, is to look at your "misfortune" as a test. That's right: a test of your strength. Remember, this is not something that you called upon yourself, but it will now become one of the many tests that you will learn something from and live through.

In relation to stress management, I believe that one of the greatest resources an individual can possess is the ability to embrace change, both positive and negative. This becomes the essence of stress resilience.

So, daring to be different requires a shift in the way we will approach any change, whether it's reacting to a situation or initiating a new way of behaving and thinking.

> One definition of insanity is doing the same thing over and over and expecting different results. The reality is that we must change and become more flexible in order to fully survive. This essentially requires for us to be different in our approaches and reactions to the changing world.

A research team once came up with a remarkable study concerning mental adjustments to cancer. They found that a patient's coping style could be grouped into four categories. These approaches were so dramatic that people could almost see the mind-body interaction.

➤ **Fighting Spirit:** Fully accepts the diagnosis, adopts an optimistic attitude, seeks information about cancer, and is determined to fight the disease.

➤ **Denial:** Either rejects the diagnosis or denies or minimizes its seriousness.

➤ **Stoic Acceptance:** Accepts the diagnosis, does not seek futher information, and adopts a fatalistic attitude.

➤ **Helplessness/Hopelessness:** The patient is engulfed by knowledge of the diagnosis and life is disrupted by preoccupation with cancer and dying.

After five years, individuals categorized as "fighting spirit" had an 80 percent survival and wellness outcome, while 70 percent of the "deniers" were alive and well. Those in the categories of "stoic" or "helpless/hopeless" had a less favorable outcome, with 37 percent and 20 percent survival rates, respectively. Grouped together, the fighters and deniers were more than twice as likely to be alive and well five years later than those in the other two groups.

Learned helplessness was originally studied with dogs. When they were placed on one side of a divided box, the dogs quickly learned to leap over a small dividing wall to the other side to avoid an electrified floor. If they were given a warning prior to the shock, most of the dogs learned to avoid the shock by leaping the barrier before the shock arrived.

Some of the dogs were placed in a harness and were given several painful shocks. The animal was trained to be helpless to escape these shocks. When they were placed in a similar box as the above dogs, none attempted to escape, but whined, crouched and howled. Through prior conditioning, they had already learned that nothing could be done to avoid the shock.

So, helplessness occurs when events appear to be uncontrollable. Individuals who are made to feel helpless in one situation are more likely to act helpless in other situations. This similarity between learned helplessness and depression, or not daring to be different, is very strong.

The good news is HOPE! Seligman found that if he forcibly dragged the helpless dogs away from the shock and into the safe environment several times, the animals gain more control over their environment. When these animals are given mastery training over their environment, they eventually become more resistant to learned helplessness.

"Most men lead lives of quiet desperation"
Thoreau

We get stuck into a familiar life of routines. It is normal and easy to fall into a level of complacency. We habituate and get stuck very easily.

Being predictable within a predictable environment helps us feel comfortable.

Routine patterns of behavior and thought eventually become habit, and then we become suspicious of those who deviate from our own way of behaving. Examples: driving the same way to a destination time and time again, shaving the same way, engaging in redundant irrelevant dialogue, etc.

The feeling of anxiety is the fear that arises from unknown future events. We are enculturated to believe that we must always worry about something. We must alter our routines of thought and behavior in order to become unstuck. Unfortunately, it is too often a crisis that forces an individual to change and adapt.

This can be observed when someone is given a life-threatening challenge. In Lawrence LeShan's poignant book, "Cancer As A Turning Point," story after story is filled with individuals who confront their illnesses, psychologically learning new methods of adaptation and consciously routing their immune system onto a course of healing. Prior to the diagnosis, life was business as usual. Forced to confront and later modify their existence through health-promoting thoughts, behaviors and medical treatment, they triumphed! LeShan, who is considered the pioneer of cancer psychotherapy, walks people through the journey of recovery and hope.

The final analysis comes from mobilizing the individual's own self-healing abilities along with advanced treatments from the medical community.

"Whatever you can do, or dream, you can begin it.
Boldness has genius, power and magic in it."
W.H. Murray

Being different means stepping out into unknown possibilities and fears. Confronting your uniqueness will bring you up against four new issues:

1.   It will create a new self-image and a shift in your self-concept.
2.   People will treat you differently and possibly resist the new you.
3.   You will have to take on new demands and responsibilities.
4.   You may get everything you really want.

The true test of a strong mentor is how well he or she is able to handle a situation that has turned into a crisis. True leadership is not tested when all is moving along as predicted, but when the tides change and chaos erupts. True leaders will rise and navigate through the turbulence.

One of the most avant-garde, daring-to-be-different to fulfill his mission, was Nelson Mandela. He is revered everywhere as a vital force in the fight for human rights and racial equality. Based on his fighting spirit, and his history of being oppressed, which included being imprisoned for 27 years, I am certain he had to live the significance of these words from his 1994 inaugural speech, which are insightful and inspirational for anyone who needs to believe in himself or herself:

"**Our deepest fear is not that we are inadequate.**

Our deepest fear is that we are powerful beyond measure.

Is our light, not our darkness, that which most frightens us?

We ask ourselves, who am I to be brilliant, gorgeous, talented, fabulous?

Actually, who are you not to be?

You are a child of God.

Your playing small doesn't serve the world.

There's nothing enlightened about shrinking so that other people won't feel insecure around you.

We are all meant to shine, as children do.

We are born to manifest the glory of God that is within us.

It's not just in some of us; it's in everyone.

And as we let our own light shine, we unconsciously give other people permission to do the same.

As we're liberated from our own fear, our presence automatically liberates others."

> "We forfeit three-fourths of ourselves in order
> to be like other people."
> *Arthur Schopenhaurer*

CHAPTER 11

Hello, my name is Anonymous and I have no idea why I am in this group!

"No man is an island unto himself, but all
are a part of the main." John Donne

Robert Putnam, a Harvard professor of Public Policy has recently released disheartening facts concerning socialization in America;

➤ We spend 35% less time visiting friends than we did thirty years ago.
➤ American families have dinner together only 2/3 as often as they did a generation ago.
➤ Americans sign 30% fewer petitions and are 40% less likely to join a consumer boycott as compared to a decade ago.
➤ Membership and activity in all sorts of clubs, civic and religious organizations continue to decline with the rate of attendance from 1970's to 1998, dropping by nearly 60%.
➤ Since the 1970's, church attendance has declined approximately 30%.

> ➤ Membership of organizations such as the PTA, the Elks club, League of Women Voters, the Red Cross and other similar voluntary organizations has declined 25-50% over the last two to three decades.
> ➤ The growth of volunteers over the last ten years is due almost entirely to increasing volunteering by retirees from the "long civic generation" not from the upcoming generation.

Social support is on the decline because of the time pressures of two career families; there are more single and childless people; suburban sprawl; electronic entertainment; baby boomers, Generation X-ers and Y-ers are less engaged in community life. We must each find that special balance between solitude and relationships with others. Some of us – the introverts – need time away from others in order to recharge our batteries. It's not just OK; it's good and necessary. Others of us – the extroverts – draw energy from others. That's OK, too. Decide where your balance lies, and ask your loved ones to respect your needs – while you offer to do the same for them.

There is great strength in numbers. Don't go it alone. As you increase the number of people involved in a project, any project, you will create the energy needed to find a solution or simply live through your current crisis.

In working through the tectonic plate stresses rubbing up against us at work and at home, there are two approaches you can take: problem-focused coping and emotion-focused coping. Problem-focused can said to be external – you change what you are doing in response to a problem. Emotion-focused is more internal – how you feel about what's going on around you. In both approaches, it helps to make conscious, positive-based decisions.

> The extremely strong effects of relationships on the quality of experience suggest that investing energy into relationships is a great way to improve one's life.

In a not so obvious sort of way, there are beneficial effects derived from a bunch of guys sitting around watching sports. It's the shared interest and socially appropriate companionship that they are experiencing. Taken another step, if you have spent any time at those adrenaline charged multilevel marketing functions or all day motivational seminars. I think you know what I mean Mr. AMWAY and Ms. Mary Kay! The attendees drive away feeling as if they are connected with others and they can take over the world with their new secret ideas. Being a part of the whole is how they experience the group gathering.

The research setting was in a maternity unit in Guatemala. The experimental treatment involved the presence of an untrained laywoman who stayed with an expectant mother during labor. She provided social support for the mother through conversation and physical touch. She did not provide professional care. The results of the study were striking. The mothers in the treatment group had shorter labor (8.8 versus 19.3 hours), they were more awake after delivery and they stroked, smiled, and talked to their babies more than the other mothers. The researchers reasoned that this type of social support helped to reduce the anxiousness of the mothers.

David Spiegel of Stanford University randomly assigned 86 women with metastatic breast cancer to a control group or a supportive therapy group. Patients in both groups received standard medical treatment for breast cancer. In addition, the therapy group met weekly for one year to receive psychological support as well as training for pain control. Patients in the therapy group lived an average of 18 months longer than those in the control group and this difference held even after taking into account how advanced the cancer was at the time it was diagnosed and in treatment regimens.

David Jones studied Vietnam veterans who had been POWs for at least six years. Guilt and loss of self-esteem were major problems for these men when they were pushed beyond their endurance limits when they were interrogation. Jones found that the healthiest survivors were in camps in which prisoners developed intense loyalty and support from one another and who understood and forgave those who leaked the information when they were being tortured.

Nearly 7,000 residents in Alameda California responded to an extensive questionnaire on personal health and other characteristics. Upon examination of the data several years later, researchers found that social ties had the highest correlation with health and longevity. People with many close social ties had a risk of death that was low, relative to people with few social ties. Social isolation was a clear risk factor. The study further showed that men and women who had close social ties were less likely to get cancer and were at a much lower risk of dying when diagnosed.

In a replication of the Alameda study conducted with nearly 3,000 in Tecumseh, Michigan, the ten-year study found that social ties had the highest correlation with health and longevity. Individuals with close social ties lived longer than those who lacked them.

Taking this one step further, a small Italian-American community in eastern Pennsylvania was studied because they had an unusually low death rate from myocardial infarction. The Rosetans had no heart-related deaths for people under the age of 47 for 6 years. The death rate from heart attacks was half that of neighboring communities and of the United States as a whole. They were overweight, consumed more fat than the average American, smoked a lot, lived a sedentary life and average cholesterol levels. The low number of heart attacks was not due to their diet, ethnic or genetic factors, but to the mutual support they gave one another, especially during a time of crisis.

The citizens of Roseto's neighboring town, Bangor, had a death rate that was equal to the national average. Those in Bangor were not ethnically uniform, did not maintain cultural traditions, did not participate in social affairs, and were not mutually supportive during crises. Then the researchers predicted that as the Rosetans became more Americanized, their social support system would break down and heart related disorders would approach the national average. The prediction came true as their cultural structure began to dissolve.

CHAPTER 12

Mothers, fathers and the search for ourselves.

THE SPAN OF THE HUMAN CYCLE
(HISTORY) Pre-Birth—Infancy—Early Childhood—
Childhood—Adolescence—Young Adulthood—Adulthood—
Middle Age—Old Age—Afterlife (LEGACY)

Two monks vowed to silence, solitude and celibacy were on a daylong journey from one monastery to another. At the beginning of their journey, they came upon a woman who was attempting to cross a wide and fast river. She kindly asked one of the monks if he would carry her across because she was not able to make it on her own. Without a word, the older monk picked her up and made the trek across the powerful stream and placed her on the other side of the river. She thanked him and then she and the monks went down different roads.

As the sun set at the end of the day, the younger monk asked, "Brother, why is it you carried that woman across the river earlier this morning? I do not understand."

"Well, my young brother, after I carried her across the river, I left her on the bank. Why is it that you could not – and instead have been carrying her with you all day?"

It would make our lives so much easier if we could be like the older monk and leave our past behind. For good or ill, we all carry the past with us, while much of it should be left at the banks of rivers we have already crossed.

It was Albert Einstein who said, "The significant problems we face cannot be solved at the same level of thinking we were at when we created them."

> **The single most important, as well as most difficult, task for an adult is to learn to accept yourself, just the way you are.**

In a society that over-glamorizes the individual spirit, we instead become seduced into believing that we have to be like others, our idols, in order to live out our true selves. It was E.E. Cummings who wrote, "To be nobody-but-yourself in a world which is doing its best, night and day, to make everybody else—-means to fight the hardest battle which any human being can fight, and never stop fighting."

We end up becoming disconnected from who we really are and what we really want. We begin to see that others have it, we don't have it and with some magic, we will finally be there, fulfilling our dream.

Commercialization's main focus is on sex and relieving some form of anxiety. The focus is to mislead us into believing that we are "not quite good enough," but with the right ingredient, we will succeed! It conforms the individual to be among the many who believe that they are unique and individualistic.

The real pride in parenting comes when our children go beyond our own fears and fantasies, find their own path, and fully live out their true potentials. When they have overcome our anxieties, not theirs.

It becomes the dilemma of the authenticity of who we are.

By being a unique individual, you will find that everyone will not like you. But the more uniqueness to your personality, the more you will find others gravitate around you who appreciate your uniqueness.

Through the broad similarities in the universal stages of life, we all pass through with important lessons. As we navigate through each of these developmental milestones, we will be confronted with difficult tasks. If we are able to successfully master each of these tests, this will give us greater possibility to move through life, relatively equipped for the struggles that we will inevitably encounter. Failure to conquer each stage can set us up for a more difficult future — but not always.

Childhood is an extended period of time where we are completely dependent upon our caregivers for nutrients to survive. Not just food and water, but love, trust, security, self-control, freedom, rules of society, and guidance for handling success as well as failure.

After being released from the dizzying questions of adolescence — especially the essential one of "Who am I and how do I fit in"? —

Through young and middle adulthood the focus becomes forming significant meaningful relationships, focusing on the development of your own children and building the foundation for a satisfying career.

Late adulthood becomes a time of contemplation as one looks back over life with acceptance and meaning. The person who has lived a full moral life has internal integrity, and the aging process is faced with greater dignity.

During this extremely influential trail of childhood, we become imprinted with the foundation of who we believe we are. Folks who did not have instructional manuals on the most effective method of parenting nurtured us. Their lessons were passed down through countless generations. It still makes me somewhat nauseous when consoling friends will tell you, "Well, they were doing the best they could." Gee, I guess that makes a lot of sense, if you believe it! If you are one of the very few who believes it!

These gods (Mommy and Daddy) were the architects of our character. Right or wrong, they developed the plans for our sense of "aliveness."

Some of us are carrying around baggage about the unresolved childhood issues of failing to forgive and respect our parents for what they did. For those who have been able to achieve this level of acceptance, strong development will take place. For the rest of us, remaining hatred and resentment toward our parents is just plain bad for us, especially as we age. We may somehow feel justified to hold onto these resentments, but it only hurts us.

To become fully human, to grow up, is the ability to accept your parents for who they were or are, and what they were attempting to accomplish, to release the internal burden of anger and being stuck in the past.

Tolstoy wrote, "All happy families are alike, but an unhappy family is unhappy in its own unique way."

It can become rationally realistic to see how destructive some families were to their children, from abandonment to engulfment to incest. This type of abuse, as well as other unique forms, creates a hollow existence for the one carrying it around with them. The damage is profound and deep. The depths of the emotional scars will become evident later in life when they make attempts to form intimate relationships with others.

As adults, our awakening process will begin when we are able to see the "creators" as also less-than-perfect beings who gave us life. They brought us in and, at times, fumbled through the rearing process with their numerous shortcomings. So there it is and now it will come down to the choice of freeing yourself so that you may live.

We owe it to ourselves to live.

Why is it that so many people have such strong feelings (positive and negative) about their mommies and daddies?

Many years ago, a psychologist by the name of Konrad Lorenz conducted an experiment on baby geese in which he became their "Mother." The result of the study made us all more familiar with the term "imprinting." Ducks or humans, here it goes. Lorenz, an ethnologist who studied animal behavior, hatched geese in an incubator and was the first object they saw when they came into the light. From then on, these baby geese followed him as if he were actually their mother.

This can be viewed as instinctive behavior, but more importantly it highlights the power of connecting with a significant other. The baby geese and the baby human have no cognitive appraisal at work when they attach. They just do!

My observations have shown me that the symbiotic connection between a mother and her son is as strong, and similar to that of a father and his daughter. What is it about this crossing of parents and their children?

It is so difficult to make a law out of human behavior and the human condition. Even with the best of theories, creating the optimal conditions for the most predictable outcome, someone will invariably break the rules of the theory. So with every stated fact about the human condition, keep in mind that it is not a fact in all cases. As predictable as we could be, we are not. Because of our uniqueness, the changing environment, unknown factors and the mystery of the future, absolutely nothing can be calculated perfectly.

It was William James, the father of American psychology, who noted that the appearance of only one white crow is needed to dispel forever the idea that all crows are black. This would be true in an idealist world, even though it can ultimately be seen as statistically insignificant. We need much more continuous evidence than one isolated event to overrule an accepted human view of behavior and perception.

So, if a single white crow did exist, for the few who saw it, then it would be understood that all crows are not black. To the rest of the culture, the 1:1 sighting of the white crow could be written off as irrelevant and unsupported in their claims. If they did not see it, then it does not exist!

During these critical and impressionable moments of infancy, childhood and beyond, neonates come into the world eager to be filled with life. They are given parents who make an earnest attempt at giving them the best parenting possible. Well, maybe "good enough" parenting. OK, maybe some of them just did a horrible job raising you.

Your primary caregivers, unless properly retrained, were giving you a watered down version of the type of parenting they had received many years ago.

As Friedrich Nietzsche once stated, "When one has not had a good father, one must create one."

The dilemma comes years later in your ability to accept the fact that they gave you life, but really had some loose wires in the nurturing of your well-being. On one hand you honor them for bringing you into the world, but on the other hand, probably the one that swatted you, you hate them with all of your being. So you become stuck within your dilemma in the search of a deeper meaning for the why of their behavior.

The lifelong movement toward the search for ourselves can be broken down under different, but yet juxtaposing, developmental lines of:

Physical
　　Intellectual
　　　　Emotional
　　　　　　Social/Family
　　　　　　　　Moral
　　　　　　　　　　Spiritual

**Or it can simply be reduced to the triad of
the mind, the body and the spirit!**

And then the ironies of all ironies is that the role models you had tried to escape from in childhood revisit you as you become older. There comes a moment of realization during young adulthood or middle age in which you begin to repeat thoughts and behaviors that your parents exhibited. The old phrase "I've become my parents" begins to invade you. It is a mixed blessing, more so when the messages you were taught were positive and growth enhancing. Yes, the past does repeat itself.

It actually becomes a quiet reassurance that you are experiencing familiar crises and will probably react in an unconscious manner. This is a perfect example of how the unconscious emerges into consciousness.

> **One of the greatest signs of internal mental health is the ability to come to terms with the past, recognize, learn, possibly forgive, accept and then move on.**

History has shown that winners overcame tough times;
Albert Einstein could not read until he was seven.
He was called a slow learner, retarded and uneducable.
Beethoven's music teacher said that he was hopeless as a composer.
He composed his greatest works after becoming deaf.
Edison's teacher labeled him unable to learn.
He tried over 2,000 experiments before he got the light bulb to work.
Winston Churchill failed the sixth grade.
Helen Keller seemed "irredeemable."
Abraham Lincoln was raised in poverty.

James Earl Jones stuttered so badly that he communicated with written notes.

Itzhak Perlman was paralyzed from the waist down since the age of four.

Franklin Delano Roosevelt was stricken with polio.

General Douglas MacArthur was accepted to West Point the third time he tried.

Woody Allen failed motion picture production at New York University and City College of New York, as well as flunking English.

So, there are many roads to becoming a successful and mature adult who contributes to the world. There are many presumably "wrong" turns to take, many destructive memories of the past, as well as several different places to end up. The idea that there is one paradigm for reaching adulthood through perfect parenting, or perfect circumstances, is not true now, nor has it ever been!

With the inherent vicissitudes of the human condition, the best we can all do is teach through love and support. We may all be flailing through, but that does not make us sick and/or abnormal or dysfunctional.

CHAPTER 13

Men, Women, Mars, Venus, toilet paper and toothpaste

(Or much ado about nothing)

"It is not our purpose to become each other;
it is to recognize the other, to learn to see the
other and honor him for what he is."
Hermann Hesse

Yada, yada, yada, blah, blah, blah, he said and she said!

From the supermarket check out stands to prime time TV and radio talk shows, we are all becoming more fascinated and ill informed about the real mystery between the sexes. And with the over-abundance of information, we become less knowledgeable about the inherent puzzle that exists in the gap between men and women.

Overall, the types of people who enjoy remaining stuck on this level of conversation are superficial and stuck in Levels #1 and #2 of a shallow existence. But, boy does this shallowness of external beauty and shiny happy personalities sell!

It is a wonderful life as a man!
It is a wonderful life as a woman (so I've heard).
And then the two intersect and the confusion exists.

We are born with instinctual natures and societal norms shape us into the kinds of men and women we need to be, in order to survive as civilized people. Learning sex role behavior begins immediately after we enter into the world. The young neonates are held differently, played with differently, given different play toys and base colors, as well as different levels of freedom and expectations.

The little boys are taught goal-directed behaviors and the suppression of their emotional nature, while the girls are encouraged to express through emotion-oriented behaviors. There is an attempt to raise our little loves this way in order to function in the world more effectively.

Even though this may make us feel more competent, in the end, it sets up an imbalance that hinders us.

This reminds me of the story about the scorpion and the frog.

A scorpion had done as much damage as he could on the east side of a stream. Eyeing the west side and his strong desires to hunt and be feed, he came upon a potential victim, the frog. He began to plead with the frog to let him get a ride on his back in order to make his way to the other side of the stream.

The frog was amazed at the request, stating the fact that the scorpion has been pre-wired to kill him. The scorpion replied that this may be true, but gave his word that he would not, under any circumstances, kill his traveling companion. Arguing back and forth, the frog was reassured that the scorpion would set him free and not kill him after his job was fulfilled.

As they traveled across the stream, the promise was kept. Just as they reached the shore on the west side, the scorpion swung his tail around and stuck the deadly needle into the frog's side.

As the frog lay dying, he requested an explanation from his foe.

The scorpion calmly replied, "I'm sorry, it's just my nature, I couldn't control it!"

Here are two interesting observations I encountered. Of course these are only two of thousands, but they are two that genetically and culturally hit the mark!

During a recent out-of-town trip I was reminded of this male/female dilemma, as well as how insensitive and amoral some men can be. I stopped at a convenience station to fill up the car and eat some microwaveable food filled with yummy preservatives (which, I presume, will make me live longer. That's what preservatives do, right?). The date was the fifth of May, which I then recalled was Cinco de Mayo. This is an official holiday that gives otherwise calm and civil people the opportunity to drink excessive amounts of beer, act like fools and do really, really, really stupid things. I wonder if we even know why we celebrate this holiday.

A young man was conversing with the checkout lady with two 12-packs of some highly overrated beer on the counter. The lady was professionally pleasant as she informed him what his total was for the beer. The young man did his job very well as he pulled out the impressive wad of money and propositioned her. "Hey honey, it's Cinco de Mayo and we're havin' a party at our place. Do you want to come over? What time do you get off?"

She very calmly said, "Well I'm married, eight months pregnant and I don't get off until 11:30."

"That's cool", he said excitedly "We'll still be partying then; we're going all night. So do you want to come over and have some beer?"

"Remember that I told you that I am married and I can only drink orange juice because I'm eight months pregnant."

"Man, that's really a bummer that you can't drink beer. Do you still want to come over?"

"May I help the next customer please?"

"OK then, I'll see you at 11:30?"

Let's not reduce all man and female interactions to this primitive ape. Maybe he just couldn't resist his animal urges, or maybe he was just a sexist, insensitive jerk-face. And to be equally balanced, here is an encounter with the other sex.

A young girl grows up, graduates from formal schooling and biologically feels the need to marry and have children. She finds her perfect man (is this another oxymoron?) and weds in bliss. They form a family and the rules of the relationship change. This, she learns, is a completely normal part of the life span.

Later, as she begins her career, she feels a type of emptiness about her life and a sort of depression sets in. Because of the walls that have developed with her husband over the years, she establishes relationships with her co-workers.

One peer, especially, finds the ability to tap a deeper, empathic cord with her and they become closer. Her co-worker begins to give her the ability to express herself in a way that is comforting and fulfills a part of her that she knew was missing. With much soul searching and support of her friends, she justifies her decision to leave the family and trek out on her own. Well, not completely on her own, but with her new igniter.

What we all need more of is compassion and appreciation; maybe attempting to gain understanding is way too much for our biased cerebral cortexes.

What's all this fuss about attempting to understand what is going on with the opposite gender? Well, it sure has become an obsession with very little real understanding or enlightenment.

Maybe this is because the average number of times a married couple engages in lovemaking is 1.2 times per week. Maybe because of all the TV commercials that point out our lack of gender appreciation and the medications we can consume to make everyone blissfully, physically and emotionally content.

Or maybe it was the sex researcher who said that men have some sort of sexual thought every 7 seconds. No wonder we have such a bad reputation for being so narrow minded. Has 7 seconds passed yet?

Maybe it's because we really don't know and will never know! But the wonder of the mysterious is alluring.

A friend of mine who is a pastor of a large congregation told me of a familiar and repetitive marital tale. The husband and wife come in for consultation. Their marriage overall is fine (whatever that is supposed to mean) but they have a never-ending source of tension over two extremely important issues: *toilet paper* and *toothpaste*. (I would like to also include the whole dilemma surrounding the toilet seat placement.) I guess there is a certain way that the toilet paper needs to roll from the front of the dispenser or the back. And then there is a proper way to squeeze and cap the toothpaste tube. Now tell me why everything seems to end up in the bathroom?

Men vs. women explained:

Fact #1—-We think about different things.

Fact #2—We need different things in order to be satisfied.

Fact #3—-We will be driven to obtain these "things."

Fact #4—-We will never be the same and should not attempt to be.

Fact #5—-Few of us will ever reach any level of complete satisfaction with our partners, let alone ourselves.

Fact #6—-It is not, and will not, ever be equal or fair.

"When women are depressed, they either eat or go shopping. Men invade another country. It's just a whole different way of thinking."
Elaine Boosler

Men and women communicate, which is the essence of all human interaction, at different levels of expectancy. Beyond the obvious physical differences, this is our most basic division.

Women will talk for the sake of connecting. There does not need to be a reason, let alone a need to come up with definitive conclusions to their interactions.

Men will talk for the sake of the completion of a problem. If we are talking, there must be a reason for it. This means that there is a problem and we need to find the most realistic solution to it!

What's really important is that we find ways to communicate in an understandable manner. Every couple develops their own form of non-verbal and verbal relating. What is just as important is the way in which we talk to each other.

Let me now refer to Eric Berne and his dissection of forms of communication between each other. Transactional analysis is based on a relatively simplistic theme (my favorite kind). He said, similar to Freud, that our personalities have three basic parts, or ego states of relating. They are termed the Child, the Adult and the Parent. Each "state" contains unique behaviors, words, tones, gestures, attitudes, expressions and overall disposition.

The Child is a product of our youth, which is primitive, impulsive, demanding, creative, playful and manipulative.

The Adult is a mature and rational decision-making entity of the personality.

The Parent is the internal "Taping" of all the messages received from the parents and/or primary care givers as the personality was forming.

The recognition of these three types can be related to the way in which we interact with others. What state do we fall into (child, adult, or parent)? Serious problems will erupt in relationships when we begin to cross the states in which we relate.

If all adult interactions remained in an Adult-to-Adult state, few problems would exist. When an encounter between two adults crosses lines — that is, one adult assumes the authoritarian parental role as he/she speaks to the other as if speaking to a child — these little less-than-obvious games that people play can turn into emotionally and physically destructive forces.

The implications of these three styles of communicating can also be witnessed within the work environment. At times it is very obvious and just as destructive.

Another interesting and troubling concept around the male/female thing is that we are somehow incomplete unless we have a significant other in our lives. As if it is an unspoken belief that if you are alone you are less than a full-functioning human being. Now this makes a lot of sense, doesn't it?

Frankly, there are some people who are more content without another attached to their sides. They have made a conscious choice, for any number of reasons, to remain that way.

The three driving qualities that are essential in a close relationship are Intimacy, Passion, and Commitment. When the bond is threatened, one of the key qualities falls short of the expectations. The healthier the bond, the closer these three are connected. Keep in mind that in the life of a long-term mental and physical link, we will move in and out of closeness we experience. This is natural and should be expected.

The most successful relationships are those that are able to handle the conflicts that will naturally erupt (in every healthy/normal relationship). If two people form any type of bond, conflicts of all types are inevitable. Not all couples handle conflict in the same way. Here are four types of resolution styles — one is not better than the other, and they are what they are. Who is to judge what is really acceptable within one's interpersonal interactions?

Validating—-the one that seems to be the most normal (ideal?) is that compromise is the end result with both parties relatively satisfied.

Volatile—-passionate disputes arise as a result of the shared conflict.

Conflict avoiding—the confrontation of the sensitive issues are dealt with and "agree to disagree" is the status quo.

Silence is golden—-the couples remain distant and non-communicative.

The reality is that there are no truly normal relationships due to the fact that every dynamic between two people is the only one of its kind. The best one can work toward, and it is work on each person's part, is to reach what is summarized in Chapter # 16 on power. The main attributes are trust, honesty, respect, the ability to communicate, positive attitude, humor, to put the other first, to give credit to the other, compromise — all the qualities we know are great.

Finding and remaining with the one that connects with you has many interesting implications. The strongest appears to be that this other has a very familiar history. Namely, you have just reconnected with your mommy or daddy. I'm sure stranger things have happened in the course of human history, but this is a repeating pattern.

We marry into familiar territory. We couple with the models we were raised by. This is why familiarity breeds contempt! Not only do we begin to talk like our parents, we come to realize that we have also married them.

What is also just as fascinating is that issues in past relationships that are unresolved come back to remind us that more work needs to be done. This can be seen when individuals jump from one relationship to another without the proper time to mourn, learn and heal from past performances. Multiple marriages will have multiple partners in their beds during the life of a current significant relationship.

Everything I ever need to know about men and women I learned at a Bob Dylan concert. The essentials of understanding the complexities of the man/woman thing came to me as I was witnessing an extraordinary event, Bob Dylan singing. Or at least he was mumbling through the lines of songs that were so familiar to me that I was glad I knew the words by heart. The music and tone of the Dylan man were out of synch with the way that I grew up listening to this incredible lyrical genius.

So anyway, back to my wife. There we were at the concert, when I realized the mystery between men and women. Here is how the rules unfolded — and by the way, thank you, again, Bob Dylan.

Rule #1-We all make sacrifices

Rule #2-We all must compromise

Rule #3-We all must recognize and acknowledge to each other the sacrifices and compromises we make

Rule #4-Sometimes it is better to go along and support the other

Rule #5-Relationships will never be equal and fair, but you can at the very least make an attempt.

Rule #6-I can sing better than Bob Dylan (this rule is, of course, universal)

It also becomes a fascinating discussion topic when several times a year a crack medical research team has spent someone else's money to come up with another biological difference between the sexes. Some small chemical within the brain or an organ/gland that is larger or smaller with the animal. This is reassuring to us all, giving us another rationalization to why we behave as we do.

Maybe we all need to revisit a paper that was published several years ago in a distinguished journal of social psychology. Delineating all of the possible factors relating to a healthy marriage, the researchers came up with a surprising finding. If the man said only two words to his wife, the marriage would survive. Those two words were, "Yes dear."

Taken one step further, I suggest that it can work both ways. Men and women can both repeat these magical words to each other and the world would be a more beautiful place. So let's try this simple exercise in communication now, "**YES, DEAR.**" These two words could add years on to the health of your life.

The overriding impression I want to leave with you is this: "Yes, dear!" Think of the other first, and your needs next. Do what is best for the other's growth and development and the result will most likely be that they will do the same for you.

The mystery is no longer a puzzle if you do what is best for your partner! Theorists can give you some relatively constructive ideas about relationships, but they will not focus in on the specific dynamics of your special dance. The dance is the unique relationship that has grown between the individuals.

So, in the final analysis of the differences that will continually be there, the wisest lesson we can derive is that of pure and unadulterated appreciation for each other — a loving, unconditional and full-hearted support of the existence of another's life and desires.

Nietzsche said, "You have your way. I have my way. As for the right way, the correct way, and the only way, it does not exist." So no more ridiculous articles about men and women.

As Forrest Gump so simplistically stated, "And that's all I have to say about that!"

CHAPTER 14

How To Become The Ultimate Athlete

I have a magic pill that you have probably seen on a poorly orchestrated infomercial. But this magic pill will require work on your part, which no longer makes it a magic pill.

And the pill of the day is — exercise!

Another annual national report has been released pointing out that Americans are once again overweight and out of shape. We are becoming increasingly more sedentary with each passing year and each generation. Our comfortable lifestyle along with increased automation is making our physical movement more restricted and as a result, we all suffer in the long run.

This pill called exercise is actually a panacea for many of our common ills. The human body is designed for an active life. There are countless scientific articles that report a direct link between physical activity and good mental *and* physical health.

Here are three points to fall back on in your attempt to become the ultimate athlete:

1). Do not attempt to be the ultimate athlete. Do what it takes to be satisfied.

2). Experiment to find the "right" routine and rhythm that suits your mental and physical needs at this point in your life.

3). Go beyond your excuses and make it a habit.

Almost any form of exercise is the key in maintaining a vibrant body and mental sharpness. It is not necessary to be an ultimate athlete; you need not engage in a vigorous exercise routine to obtain the lifelong benefits of working out. More exercise could improve your overall performance, but for the beginner, even a little makes a gigantic difference in the quality of your life.

Three factors to consider in establishing an exercise program:

i.   Frequency—how often (4 to 5 times a week)

ii. Intensity—how difficult (as monitored by heart rate and breathing)

iii. Duration—how long (at least ½ hour)

As you design your exercise routine, keep in mind that an effective workout will physically stimulate the heart, lungs and major muscle groups. You will also have to differentiate between the current workout fads and the one that will eventually fit your mental and physical profile.

The two most difficult portions of an exercise program are the courage to begin, and then creating the habit. It will take approximately 4 weeks of regular exercise before your new conditioning program will no longer be a struggle. But again, it is the first four weeks of the development of the new habits that are the most difficult. One of the greatest athletes of all time and a winner of the dreaded Hawaiian Ironman Triathlon (2.4 mile swim, 112 mile bike and 26.2 mile run) once commented on his most difficult training obstacle. He said that the hardest part of his workout schedule was walking out the front door every morning to get started; after that it was easy.

Research has indicated that one of the strongest predictors of an individual's happiness, optimistic mental state and satisfaction with life, is being aerobically fit. Combining the physiological benefits of a good exercise program, along with the psychological side effects, results in the production of an incredible stress resilient human being.

So, what about the psychological effects of exercise?

- The most naturally effective form of stress release.
- Clarity of thought and sharpness of focus.
- Creates a peaceful state of mind.
- A time of solitude and reflection.
- Reduces the episodes and/or intensity of depression, anxiety and a wide variety of psychosomatic disorders.
- Increase in self-esteem and body self-concept.
- Endorphines and other natural mind-altering chemicals are stimulated and released.

Just as in concepts of motivation, there are easier and quicker ways to achieve a machine that operates in peak performance, but these are not as effective. I am concerned with our quick fix, faster-and-bigger is-better, drive-through, want-it-now-and-I-want-it-all mentality. Medication and instrumentation can give you it all, right now. This comes to be a shallow approach to the whole act of exercising. Remember the journey is the journey, not the destination. It is how to get there, not that you are there.

Rod had just finished a long week of work. He just phoned his wife and 2-year-old daughter from the corporate parking lot, letting them know that he would be home in a few minutes. He loved his family and he loved his work. Rod had everything he could ask for. He was part of the wiz upper management for a very large communications company in Kansas City. Just as he finished the call, started his car, and began the short journey home, he leaned over his steering wheel and died. He was only 32 years old!

Was it his diet, lack of exercise, lack of love and humor, genetic predisposition for his condition or possibly a hopeless pessimist? Wrong on all accounts! His time had come.

Rod and his wife had a passion for exercise, as well as having a lot of fun. One of Rod's dreams that he was building up for was to qualify and participate in the Hawaiian Ironman Triathlon.

Rod's wife Rachel picked up his dream after he died. Juggling a busy corporate schedule, raising a child and attempting to take care of herself, she put the wheels in motion (literally). She rose early in the morning before her daughter awakened from her slumber to work out and also squeezed in an occasional evening sweat. A baby monitor hooked up next to her treadmill and stationary bike kept her connected to her sleeping daughter upstairs.

She had developed an even stronger support network of extended family and friends, which aided her in her mission. She spent approximately 25 hours a week pushing her physical and emotional limits as she pursued her goal.

With a dream to focus on, a lot of determination and the desire to overcome adversity, she qualified and completed the grueling triathlon in *only* 13 hours and 15 minutes.

But she didn't stop there! She became the president of Widow Person's Services in Denver and writes for an international magazine on grief in the workplace. Rachel has published a manual for employers for dealing with death and grief in the workplace.

Get started, because there is an extremely large gap between knowing and doing. Now you know; now go do it!

CHAPTER 15

The real secret behind motivation is no secret at all.

It was Winston Churchill who said, "Continuous effort — not strength or intelligence — is the key to unlocking our potential." Well, there it is! Motivation is the *action* that precedes success.

"You already possess everything necessary to become great."
Crow Indian Proverb

The following words were written on the tomb of an Anglican bishop in the crypts of Westminster Abbey:

"When I was young and free and my imagination had no limits, I dreamed of changing the world. As I grew older and wiser, I discovered the world would not change, so I shortened my sights somewhat and decided to change only my country.

But it too seemed immovable.

As I grew into my twilight years, in one last desperate attempt, I settled for changing only family, those closest to me, but alas, they would have none of it.

And now as I lay on my deathbed, I suddenly realize: If I had only changed myself first, then by example I would have changed my family.

From their inspiration and encouragement, I would then have been able to better my country and, who knows, I may have even changed the world."

Another way to view this is a quote from psychologist Carl Rogers, the originator of Client-Centered Therapy who wrote in "Personal Thoughts on Teaching and Learning," "I have come to feel that the only learning which significantly influences behavior is self-discovered, self-appropriated learning."

> **In this world there are only three kinds of people:**
> **Those who make things happen,**
> **Those who watch things happen,**
> **And all the rest who wondered how it all happened.**

Remember the story of the excited elementary school children who were given the task of finding out what made a frog live? As they began cutting up the frog and analyzing the pieces, the frog slowly died.

Attempting to break down what motivates individuals is a lot like the school children. Many factors are at work in motivating someone. And as far as mysteries of the human psyche go, we have just entered into another vast area of the unknown. Some factors will never be discovered.

In the best of all possibilities, you would want to do everything that was good for you. This is an inner drive that would inspire you to exceed. Most people, sadly, lack such inner motivation.

What motivates people to perform is so unclear. Even though humans are self-propelled, naturally motivated organisms, why is it that we cannot find that special ingredient to generate drive in all?

Let me begin my approach by sharing two quotes from unknown authors:

"Most people will do anything for their
own advancement except work for it."
"Nobody is going to save us; everything is left purely to the
individual, the commitment to who we are. Gurus or
spiritual friends might instigate that possibility, but fundamentally
they have no function!"

Motivation refers to the dynamics of behavior, the process of initiating, sustaining and directing activities of the organism.
- Extrinsic Motivation—stems from obvious external factors, such as money, "material things", body image, external perception of self-esteem or happiness, etc...
- Intrinsic Motivation—occurs when there is no obvious external reward or ulterior purpose behind your actions. The activity is an end in itself.

Many motivated activities can be thought of as beginning with a need. Needs cause a psychological state or feeling called a drive to develop. Drives activate a response designed to attain a goal that will satisfy the need. Meeting the need temporarily ends the motivational sequence.

Most theories agree that motivation involves these basic processes:
1. The individual is energized and there is a change of the energy level to a perceptibly higher state.
2. This increased energy is directed at a specific target (goal, objective or outcome) through a channel, mechanism or process.
3. Knowing its "triggering mechanism," its intensity or strength, and its direction or the goals toward which it is aimed.

For motivated behavior to occur, according to most theorists, three conditions must be met:
1. They must be capable of the behavior.

2. They must have the opportunity, and in some cases be encouraged by the environment, to behave in a certain way.
3. They must either require something of the environment or be required by the environment to behave.

Given that intrinsic motivation stimulates achievement, especially in situations where people work independently, how might one encourage this? The consistent answers, from hundreds of studies are: First, provide tasks that challenge and trigger curiosity and secondly, avoid snuffing out people's sense of self-determination with an overuse of controlling extrinsic rewards. It is important to expect, support, challenge and inform, but if you want to encourage internally motivated, self-directed achievements, don't be overly controlling. In some cases, just leave them alone!

As an individual pursuing your own goals, keep these simple points in mind:

1. Establish a realistic plan or goal.
2. Get started, **push** yourself and strive for continuous improvement.
3. Confront your negative self-talk as well the pessimism of others. (These dialogues will invariably arise as you begin your journey)
4. Designate specific time segments to work your plan.
5. Make it your overriding passion because you've got to be **hungry**.
6. Find your mentor to give you the necessary inspiration.
7. Surround yourself with the "right" people who have the "right" mindset. The energy that people create is the domino effect.
8. Experiment and make lots of mistakes and learn from each. This continuous experimentation will expand your area of knowledge.

9.   Monitor and reward each small success because, as the Chinese proverb states, "Small changes will bring big rewards."

The person who really wants to do something finds a way;
the other kind finds an excuse.

Let's look at a fascinating story of motivation, which came down to a conscious choice. This is a story I ran across about a guy named Jerry. Jerry and his story can be a metaphor for anyone at any time at any place.

Jerry was the kind of guy you love to hate. He was always in a good mood and always had something positive to say. When someone would ask him how he was doing, he would reply, "If I were any better, I would be twins!"

He was a unique manager because he had several waiters who had followed him around from restaurant to restaurant. The reasons the waiters followed Jerry was because of his attitude. He was a natural motivator. If an employee was having a bad day, Jerry was telling the employee how to look on the positive side of the situation.

Seeing this style really made me curious, so one day I went up to Jerry and asked him, "I don't get it! You can't be a positive person all of the time. How do you do it?" Jerry replied, "Each morning I wake up and say to myself, Jerry, you have two choices today. You can choose to be in a good mood or you can choose to be in a bad mood. I choose to be in a good mood. Each time something bad happens, I can choose to be a victim or I can choose to learn from it. I choose to learn from it. Every time someone comes to me complaining, I can choose to accept their complaining or I can point out the positive side of life. I choose the positive side of life."

"Yeah, right, it's not that easy," I protested.

"Yes it is," Jerry said. "Life is all about choices. When you cut away all the junk, every situation is a choice. You choose how you react to situations. You choose how people will affect your mood. You choose to be in a good mood or bad mood. The bottom line: It's your choice how you live your life."

I reflected on what Jerry said. Soon thereafter, I left the restaurant industry to start my own business. We lost touch, but I often thought about him when I made a choice about life instead of reacting to it. Several years later, I heard that Jerry did something you are never supposed to do in a restaurant business: He left the back door open one morning and was held up at gunpoint by three armed robbers. While trying to open the safe, his hand shaking from nervousness, slipped off the combination. The robbers panicked and shot him. Luckily, Jerry was found relatively quickly and rushed to the local trauma center. After 18 hours of surgery and weeks of intensive care, Jerry was released from the hospital with fragments of the bullets still in his body.

I saw Jerry about six months after the accident. When I asked him how he was, he replied, "If I were any better, I'd be twins. Wanna see my scars?" I declined to see his wounds, but did ask him what had gone through his mind as the robbery took place.

"The first thing that went through my mind was that I should have locked the back door," Jerry replied. "Then, as I lay on the floor, I remember that I had two choices: I could choose to live, or I could choose to die. I chose to live." "Weren't you scared? Did you lose consciousness?" I asked. Jerry continued, "The paramedics were great. They kept telling me I was going to be fine. But when they wheeled me into the emergency room and I saw the expressions on the faces of the doctors and nurses, I got really scared. In their eyes, I read, 'He's a dead man.' I knew I needed to take action." "What did you do?" I asked. "Well, there was a big, burly nurse shouting questions at me," said Jerry. "She asked if I was allergic to anything. 'Yes,' I replied. The doctors and nurses stopped working as they waited for my reply. I took a deep breath and yelled, "Bullets!" Over their laughter, I told them, "I choose to live. Operate on me as if I am alive, not dead."

Jerry lived, thanks to the skill of the medical staff, but also because of his amazing attitude. I learned from him that every day we have a choice to live fully.

Attitude is a choice.
Attitude, after all, is everything!

Optimism and pessimism are both powerful forces that we are presented with in every encounter of our lives. These forces are choices! The optimistic thinkers have always generated progress. Our choice of an optimistic attitude will counter the negativity we must all realistically face.

For six decades, beginning in 1922, the famous Terman study followed a very large group (1,528) of men and women with exceptionally high IQs. The granddaddy of all life-span research revealed, among other things, that the most successful members of the group shared a special drive to succeed and achieve that had been with them from grammar school. Their desire to drive themselves was much higher, compared to others.

Even though you cannot go back to grammar school and start over with an overriding passion to achieve, you can begin the process now!

And I mean now!

Regardless of the amount of information we receive from others or the amount of love or forcefulness of others, it all comes down to self-motivation.

You must grow up and realize that you and no one else – not your boss, not Dr. Laura or the IRS, not your parents or their methods of raising you – are responsible for how your life goes. In the final analysis, you and only you can make the choice to push yourself into achieving a higher level of existence. You weigh the risks, assess your options and take the leap of faith to create a better life. The first step? Choosing your attitude, every day, in every situation. It is the final freedom, and the first step toward true independence and fulfillment.

CHAPTER 16

Power—The Ultimate Aphrodisiac

"Nearly all men can stand adversity, but if you want to test a man's
character, give him power."
Abraham Lincoln

Social psychologists have said that humans are in search of three qualities: wealth, power and prestige. But isn't it true that these three pillars of "success" have become in our culture the all-too-powerful symbols of really "making it"?

It has been said that people of genius are admired; people of wealth are envied; people of power are feared; but only people of character are trusted.

The ill effects of megalomaniacs – those who have delusions of greatness and grandeur — have been well documented, and continue to be highlighted when someone with power abuses it. The abuse of power takes place by political leaders and corporate executives, as well as the dominant one within the family. These abusive people's existence always overshadows the good that is being delivered by those who use their influence to improve the human condition. Remember, everyone wants to find out about others' dirty laundry.

Understand, and avoid, Mohandas K. Gandhi's list of the seven deadly sins:

WEALTH WITHOUT WORK
PLEASURE WITHOUT CONSCIENCE
KNOWLEDGE WITHOUT CHARACTER
BUSINESS WITHOUT MORALITY
SCIENCE WITHOUT HUMANITY
WORSHIP WITHOUT SACRIFICE
POLITICS WITHOUT PRINCIPLE

Power, success and leadership

Look, for a moment, at those three concepts as one topic. Even though a distinction can be made, I want to look at the combined implications they bring. I have conducted two extensive research projects on each of these concepts, and the results can be bundled into common threads.

When asked by a reporter what success felt like, Ralph Fiennes said, "Success? Well, I don't know quite what you mean by success. Material success? Worldly success? Personal or emotional success? The people I consider successful are so because of how they handle their responsibilities to other people, how they approach the future — people who have a full sense of the value of their life and what they want to do with it. I call people 'successful' not because they have money or their business is doing well, but because, as human beings, they have a fully developed sense of being alive and engaged in a lifetime task of collaboration with other human beings — their mothers and fathers, their family, their friends, their loved ones, the friends who are dying, and friends who are being born.

"Success?" he repeated emphatically. "Don't you know it is all about being able to extend love to people? Really! Not the big, capital-letter sense, but in the everyday. Little by little, task by task, gesture by gesture, word by word."

And then there is the pure and complete explanation of success by Ralph Waldo Emerson, who said, "To laugh often and much; to win the respect of intelligent people and affection of children; to earn the appreciation of honest critics and endure the betrayal of false friends; to appreciate beauty; to find the best in others; to leave the world a bit better, whether by a healthy child, a garden patch or a redeemed social condition; to know even one life has breathed easier because you have lived. This is to have succeeded."

Several years ago I conducted a research project into the lives of several people who displayed qualities of success and optimism. The study was limited in number, but I was pleased with the results. When the results were completed, these individuals reported that the overriding traits that they possessed were: optimistic and high self esteem, continued learning and education, the ability to have fun, honesty, integrity and respect, being flexible and open to change, persistence and determination, the encouragement of others, associate with the right people and the drive to do the best you can do each and every day.

An expanded version of the original study was finished recently with a larger group of individuals with hundreds of responses analyzed. They came from a wide spectrum of the roles; CEO's of extremely profitable organizations, CEO's from non-profits, community leaders, community volunteers, religious leaders (men/women), physicians, politicians, hospital administrators, educators, media leaders, etc... Most were recognized as powerful and successful, as well as having a good reputation among their peers.

In both studies I was given the flexibility to exclude those who displayed the qualities that would be counter-indicative of good character. These less-than-stellar attributes were: cynicism, sarcasm, being judgmental or self-righteous, anger, aggression and drug/alcohol abuse.

Winston Churchill, considered by many as the most outstanding leader of the 20th century, was once asked, "What is a man?" Reflecting for a few moments, he responded, "Man, woman — we are nothing more than worms." He paused and then, with a glint in his eye and a smile on his face, he added, "but I do believe that I am a glow worm. There is something special about me."

There was something extraordinarily special about Churchill, just as there is something very special and unique about all true leaders.

Though they display unique characteristics, and have unique challenges to overcome, they do share common traits.

Some of those qualities, in order of importance:

(Self-Qualities)

Honesty — the ability to tell it like it is, completely and bluntly, but trustworthy in words and deeds

Ability to communicate — the good news and the less than pleasant

Learning and education — ongoing and lifelong process

Positive attitude — in spite of outside challenges

Humor — at the situation and at yourself

Hard work — "there will never be a substitute for this"

Enthusiasm and passion for the task — the love of the journey because passion makes the impossible possible

Persistence and perseverance — the ability to push forward through the obstacles

Vision — a shared promise for all because leaders are dealers in hope about the future

Organization — of people, plans, places and time

Integrity — ethical principles and a good moral foundation help to behave in a way that is exemplary

Faith in higher power — God in all that is attempted

Seek and endure change — change is inevitable so we will embrace it

Intelligence — mental and emotional

Guts to be bold — the strength to make the tough decisions

Risk taker — moving into areas of the unknown

Responses that were considered directed *toward others* were placed into a category all to themselves. The great distinguished Chinese philosopher, Lao-Tsu, wrote, "Leaders are best when people scarcely know they exist, not so good when people obey and acclaim them. Fail to honor people, they fail to honor you. But of good leaders who talk little, when their work is done, the task fulfilled, the people will all say, "We did this ourselves.'"

Or as the Seneca Indian Proverb states, "He who would do great things should not attempt them all alone."

Listening to others — the ability to get genuine input through active openness by being silent

Respect for others — allowing them to aspire through appreciation

Networking with others — the ability to get along with a wide variety of people

Servant to others — this is the heart within you for their well being

Love and support— of family/parents—to help you through the tough times

Recognition of others' talents and strengths — great leaders surround themselves with brilliant individuals

Others share the credit — You initiate the process, but in the end, *they* have made it all happen

Upon closer review of these qualities, it becomes evident that these are also the qualities that exist within a relatively healthy love relationship. It becomes the same thing that partners are looking for in a relationship that is alive and growing.

Another overriding principle is that of responsibility. Responsibility is a difficult concept for some individuals to accept. In the final analysis, true leaders and successful people see that they have great responsibility, not power.

Some individuals are highly talented but suddenly fall apart when they begin to achieve a certain level of success. Lack of character is at the root of this impasse. Harvard psychologist Steven Berglas says that people who have gained great heights but lack a strong character to carry them through stressful times are going to experience disaster. He says that they will encounter one of the four A's: arrogance, aloneness, adultery and adventure seeking.

"Setting an example is not the main means of influencing others; it is the only means."   Albert Einstein

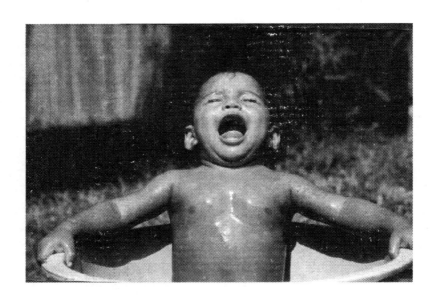

CHAPTER 17

The psychology of "IT"

Time, Action & Focus

"The least of things with a meaning is worth more in life than the
greatest of things without it."
Carl Jung

"Nothing is more likely to help a person overcome or endure troubles
than the consciousness of having a task in life."
" Happiness cannot be pursued; it must ensue."
Viktor Frankl

Hindus believe all our desires can be put into four categories, and that
they are fully attainable and accessible:

- Pleasure
- Worldly success – power, wealth and prestige
- To behave responsibly
- Liberation from obstacles on the road to complete fulfillment

All four of these paths to fulfillment can be thwarted, but the path
that trips us up the most is the fourth – because there are so many
external barriers put in our way: difficult bosses and work

environments, troubled relationships, financial pressures, political turbulence, social norms and expectations, parental influences that aren't always the best and on and on.

The first step to getting around those hurdles is awareness: recognition of the various impediments that are keeping you from being fulfilled. That is exactly the gist of this book: realizing, perhaps for the first time, what is holding you back from achieving happiness and wholeness.

In the spiral upward toward fulfillment, what you are reaching for is the "zone," self-actualization, peak experiences, peak performance, higher consciousness, enlightenment, illumination, nirvana, satori, bliss, in the groove, runner's high, on a roll, alpha-theta brain wave activity, ecstasy, aesthetic rapture. In other words…*IT.*

> **The best that we can be in the world is awake and aware.**
> **It is the purity of the present moment!**
> **That is it!**

Baba Ram Dass, who was formerly Richard Alpert when he taught psychology at Harvard University, says that, "When you carry the garbage, just carry the garbage. And bring honor to the garbage."

This may sound like some psychotic, LSD, '60s hippie-type observation, but in actuality, what he means is that our attitudes make a difference in the way we feel about a task. But garbage? Don't moan and groan about how difficult or horrible something is, just participate in it! You can bring a certain type of reverence to each and every act that you are engaged in. This would apply to every act, not just the ones that give you incredible pleasures.

This is an excellent model for everything we do in life, isn't it?

We give a deeper qualifiable meaning to every act we participate in. We unconsciously divide them into pleasure, pain, or irrelevant sensations. We quickly pass judgment on each act even before we begin the encounter.

So, taking out the trash can be an orgasmic experience if we are able to see the beauty in the experience (the ability merely to manipulate your environment; the pleasure of getting rid of waste; the opportunity to make your spouse's life just a little better – it goes on and on!). So can being stuck in traffic, confronting an uncomfortable situation, working late on a project or grounding your children for inappropriate behaviors. You truly can find magic in *everything* in this life. It is the visionaries among us who see the magic in something while the rest of us are blind to it.

Because we have a strong need to judge each act, my next suggestion may seem irrational. Don't just spend time focusing in on acts that will ensure a blissful outcome. To test your ability to see magic everywhere, choose an activity that you do not particularly enjoy, or find no joy in at all, and look for the nuggets of magic and peacefulness. They are there if you allow them to show themselves. It may be an act of enjoyment scrubbing the toilets or paying the monthly bills — find your own particular joy in every moment as it offers itself to you.

> **Weaving consciousness, time and action into every event throughout the day and then, further, throughout your life is the goal of achieving *it*! *It* is a highly alert and seamless state of mind. It requires one to remain in a state of psychological "oneness" with whatever happens, without addition or subtraction to the present act.**

Now, if you can do that, all will appear to merge into a state of fascination and tranquility. It can't hurt to try!

Whatever "it" you are doing, it is important to develop the habit of practicing the art of focused concentration. From the most simplistic tasks that are a part of your daily routine, to complicated endeavors that require all of your psychic energy. From sky diving to taking the trash out, regardless of the task, doing it with a focused awareness will bring about joy during the action.

> What I am suggesting here is a gigantic psychological leap into the realm of being caught up in the joy and awe of every single act you are engaged in. This state of existence is both probable and possible. Of course, some acts and events will be a little more full-flavored than others, but they all can be perceived and felt that way.

> *In order to achieve this state, one must adopt the mindset that you truly believe that your life is perfectly synchronized. Everything that has happened and will happen was meant to happen. So you see, all is perfection because there can be no other way for you to exist. Perfection is surrounding you and perfection is you!*

Think of it this way: You are absolutely, beautifully, uniquely, perfect at being you.

Psychic chaos, psychic entropy or internal chatter becomes the greatest obstacles to reaching this state of *it*.

Certainly, to achieve focused concentration and an ordered mental condition is not easy; otherwise, everyone would be there. Contrary to what we tend to assume, the normal state of the mind is chaos. Without training, and without an object in the external/internal world that demands attention, people are unable to focus their thoughts for more than a few moments at a time. It has been estimated that the attention span of an adult is similar to that of a child: only 6 seconds!

It **is the combination of activity, with time and focus!**

At the core of "*IT*" is being in the moment. Being lost in a moment of pure perfection. And the funniest part of this whole experience is that it is accessible to everyone; it exists at all times and it is everywhere! You need only look through the amazing porthole of a focused, optimistic, open mind.

It is a moment of pure thought, so pure that there is *no* thought, only effortless participation in a perfect act. This is an unconscious movement through an act in which nothing can go wrong, when the mind, body and spirit are one. It is in the act, for the sake of the act, and not for the sake of its outcome.

In the ancient Japanese Zen tradition, "I eat when I am hungry, I sleep when I am tired." The essence of the philosophy becomes the "everyday mind."

It is that precious moment of timelessness, where everything fades into one and all of our thoughts are pure. There is no longer time and space, there just is *it*! It is a state of awareness where there are no worries, no contradictions or conflicts, almost a state of nothingness. These are the few moments that give us an intensity of living against our earthbound level of existence.

These are the moments of effortless action.

These are monumental growth experiences when we experience *it*.

It is the fleeting moment of complete equanimity.

These are generally moments that occur when individuals are totally engrossed in their favorite activity, but it may occur at any time. It is always better to do something one feels good about than something that makes us financially better off yet emotionally and physically miserable.

Keep in mind that if one attempts to dissect the Gestalt too much, it will cease to exist. Much like the enthusiastic science students who wanted so badly to discover how a frog was able to live that they killed it. They slowly began to dissect it, and with each incision, its life began to dwindle into death. Similarly, if you get overly analytical about "it" moments, you either won't reach them or, if you do, you won't be able to sip them and savor them.

> HOW TO GET THERE, OR HOW TO BE THERE!
> NOW THIS IS A TRUE DILEMMA BECAUSE THERE ARE VERY FEW GOOD ROAD MAPS THAT WILL GET YOU THERE (OR HERE). SINCE EACH INDIVIDUAL IS DIFFERENT, EACH PATH WILL IN TURN BE DIFFERENT, BASED ON THE UNIQUENESS OF YOUR NEEDS. THE MOST REALISTIC PATH YOU CAN TAKE IS THAT OF THOSE WHO HAVE WALKED IT BEFORE. THIS IS THE WISDOM OF THE MASTERS. MASTERS IS BEING USED VERY LOOSELY BECAUSE THERE ARE MANY WHO ARE MASTERS AND PART OF THEIR MASTERY IS NOT TO DISCLOSE THAT THEY HAVE *MADE IT*.

Achieving *it* can run the continuum of participating in an ultra-endurance athletic activity to motionless forms of contemplation and relaxation. The moment of orgasm could also be considered an *it* experience, because for that brief time span, all worries and anxieties subside, the world stops and the completeness of it all is felt.

Several of these moments of pure bliss have occurred to me at different points in my life.

In a moment of irrational thought, I signed up for an eight-hour race that began with a two-mile swim in the Atlantic Ocean. Swimming is a purely peaceful activity once you get into the feel of the strokes. As I began the race, I was focused on the competition and attempting to push to the front of the pack and maintain a strong edge.

Approximately a half-mile into the race, I forgot about the competitive nature, forgot that I was swimming and just began to stare at the beauty of the ocean floor. The water was so crystal clear that the ocean floor could easily be viewed 100 feet below. An unknown amount of time had passed when I realized that I had drifted so far off course that I was unable to catch the last of the swimmers by the end of this segment of the race. Oh well, I thought to myself, that was a beautiful experience!

Another similar experience occurred when I unconsciously signed up for a 286-mile endurance race across the entire state of Missouri. I again lost track of time as well as the route that I was supposed to take. I also moved into a trance that almost caused me to be a part of several close accidents.

In exactly the same state of mind I was watching my son as he slept in his bed as a child. At that moment, which is shared by many parents, I was presented with the absolute perfection and completeness of the world. As I viewed this gift in a quiet slumber, it seemed that time, worries and worldly pursuits vanished and the face of God had his eyes closed as he waited for his own consciousness to emerge. At that moment, I felt the wholeness of life, in its state of pure perfection, with the beginning and end in absolute unity. This lasted for several minutes and then I started to worry about the normal issues all parents struggle with (his health, his future, his mother, his food, etc.).

The truth is that we need to live as if our time on Earth is limited, because it is! If you know you have only one year left to exist on Earth, what would you begin to do right now that would increase the quality of your life? Remember, it must be morally correct and the acts you participate in must make a positive impact on others.

At the risk of dissecting the frog, here's a kind of cross-section cut from the meaning of "enjoying" or "being" in each moment:

1. When we are engaged in a task that can be completed with clear goals. We are familiar with the act and the rules. From the game of chess, to complicated mathematical formulas to swimming.
2. There is a total focused concentration on the act.
3. Constant worries and frustrations dissolve, allowing thoughts to be at peace and balanced.
4. A sense of internal control while you are involved in the act
5. The concept of time dissolves into the "one" moment-now!

Or as Voltaire so elegantly put it, *"Paradise is where I am."*

When you have achieved *it*, you have just moved through several levels of awareness instantaneously:

The six levels of awareness or being

➢ The External level — size, color, age, male/female, relative beauty, ethnicity, clothing, mannerisms, sexual attractiveness or competition, the physical reality. This is the dominant superficial theme that is fueled by the marketing and advertising worlds. Because it is more important how you look than how you feel.

➢ The Psychological level — This is who I will tell you I am…..extrovert, introvert, happy, depressed, thinker, feeler, guilt, parent, child, religious, manager, artist, idiosyncrasies, democrat, republican, Kansan, etc.

➢ The Astral level——the 12 astrological signs, 12 Chinese animal signs, mythic roles, and the collective unconscious. This could be considered the biological genetic coding that has been passed down to you. This could be the strange feeling you have when you meet someone for the first time but are certain you have known of him or her before.

➢ The Multi-dimensional Soul levels — you are able to see the soul quality in another human being when you encounter them. It is an internal perception beyond Levels #1, #2, and #3. Moving deeper, you and the other can see each other's soul quality. This could be considered the spiritual realm where people of religion try to capture in others who are searching for their soul.

➢ Then, in the final #6 Level, everything moves into a non-existent, non-being, and formless state of awareness. (Now this is some heavy stuff!)

Let's end at the end, and put everything before it in perspective, with a sad but accurate statement from Ernest Becker from his life-affirming book, "The Denial Of Death":

"A person spends years coming into his own, developing his talent, his unique gifts, perfecting his discriminations about the world, broadening and sharpening his appetite, learning to bear the disappointments of life, becoming mature, seasoned-finally a unique creature in nature, standing with some dignity and nobility and transcending the animal condition; no longer driven, no longer a complete reflex, not stamped out of any mold. And then the real tragedy (is) that it takes sixty years of incredible suffering and effort to make such an individual, and then he is good only for dying."

It doesn't have to be like that at all! But it will – if we give in to the forces of negativity; if we live life on autopilot and repeat self-destructive patterns learned in childhood; if we believe the lies of the narcissists surrounding us; if we act as if life is something that just happens to us and that our lot in life is handed to us by fate.

You need not toil 60 years to make yourself into the kind of person you want to be. You're much closer than you think. And most likely, you don't need as much help as you've been led to believe.

You can do it. You can achieve *it*.

You can learn to truly live, long before it's time to die.

EPILOGUE

"The Meaning of Life"

Ladies and gentlemen, boys and girls, dudes and dudettes:
Avoid attorneys at all costs, which means always do what is morally correct. If I could offer only one tip for the future, this would be it! The long-term health benefits of avoiding these creatures have been proven by scientists, psychologists, corporations and small laboratory rats. I will dispense my best advice now, in the form of the following aphorisms and witty observations based upon years of education, training, observation and occasional idle gossip:

Do something for anyone and do not take credit for it.
Don't sweat the petty things and don't pet the sweaty things.
Never confuse your career with your life.
Spend more time enjoying each precious moment rather than worrying about the major anxiety producing concerns, such as: money, your age, your hair, your weight, your job, your future, the love you should be receiving from those who have attachments to you; or why other people appear to be so much better off than you.
Some people will never allow themselves to be happy.
It's not your lot in life to make them better off.
Everyone's got a problem.
Some have the wisdom to concentrate on the solutions.

Don't wait for things to happen; make them happen.

Happiness is an inside job, and believe me, there are many people who are jobless.

Be more concerned about how you think rather than what people think of you.

The only failures are the ones who never get beyond their fear to try.

If you fear criticism then, say nothing, do nothing, and therefore you will be nothing.

I feel compelled to mention the word sex. There! Was it good for you?

Know that success may come with a mixture of luck, but don't count on it.

Everything that is important to you is constantly changing and the amount of this change that you actually control is very small.

Listen more than you speak; that's why you have two ears and only one mouth.

Learn to be responsible and quit blaming others for your lack of responsibility.

Did I already mention the attorney part?

We are all ultimately alone.

The goal of a human being is to find out how to connect with yourself, and then with others.

Learn to love yourself because at times, you will be the only one who will.

Your true friends will always love you.

If your ego begins to get too big, find ways to reduce it. Here are some sure fire ways: try to raise children, pick your nose during an important meeting, tell the sun not to set, really look at yourself when you wake up or don't go to the bathroom for a week.

Accept that some days you're the pigeon and some days you're the statue.

It is extremely, extremely difficult to be completely honest; everyone is less than truthful, but some are more truthful than others.

People will accept your ideas much more readily if you tell them that Albert Einstein or Mark Twain said it first.

Be conscious of your prejudices. We all have them.

Learn to forgive, and then relearn to forgive when you believe there is no way you can. Forgive your parents and hope that your children will forgive you when they grow up.

Make lots of mistakes and learn from each one.

Sometimes bad things happen to good people and good things happen to bad people. There is absolutely no rational reason for it. You have a choice about what kind of a person you are going to be. In the final analysis, you are your choices.

Remember that if someone appears nice to you but he/she is rude to strangers, he/she is not a nice person.

If you find yourself alone and in the darkness of life, don't be afraid to reach out and ask someone for a light. But please, don't make it a Bud Light.

Men need to lift the seat, flush the toilet and then put the seat back down.

If you are a woman, do the same in reverse.

Laugh for no apparent reason.

Always get a second and third opinion on every major decision. In the final act, you will learn to trust your own opinion.

Nobody really cares if you can't dance well; just get up and dance.

Dance naked in front of your pets, unless you raise large carnivores.

If you have no pets, then dance naked and yell "woo woo" pretending you are a pet.

Question all cultural beliefs!

Everything that has happened and will happen to you, the good as well as the bad, is snycronistic. It was all meant to happen.

Sing often and sing loud. If you feel that you're not a good singer, just listen to Bob Dylan. How do you think he feels?

Everyone has a right to his or her opinion and a right to go to the bathroom. But, when you're in someone else's bathroom, respect his or her opinion.

True beauty has nothing at all to do with external appearance, but I would rather spend a weekend with Meg Ryan than Margaret Thatcher.

Live a simple life, so that others may simply live.

Remember that you can't take it with you, so share it while you're here.

Do not live in the world of entitlement.

No one, and I mean no one, owes you anything.

When you truly admire someone as a leader, mentor, guru, spiritual teacher, or hero, keep in mind that they are no better or worse than you. If you worship them too much, you are diminishing yourself in some way.

Nobody is normal!

No one will ever truly understand you as much as you can.

If you have ever questioned the existence of God, be patient with yourself; the questions are essential. You will eventually come to the undisputable answer.

This life is far too funny to be taken so seriously.

No matter what happens, somebody, somewhere will find a way to distort it and take it too seriously.

We have all been placed here to learn, to laugh, to love, to fully live and to leave a lasting legacy.

Each of us is a separate person. We are the subtle combinations of factors that will never occur again in history. There is only, and will only be, one of you to occupy this space and time.

If there is a beginning, then there must be an end. Everyone will eventually die. Some have gained the wisdom to fully live within this space and time. Once you find your uniqueness, then begin to live it as fully as possible.

*For a copy of this epilogue or a potential lawsuit, please contact my attorney, Mea Parasite, at the law firm of Dowe, Cheat'em and Howe.

The author

Mark Hood received his master's degree in psychology from the University of Missouri with specialized training in biofeedback and stress management from the Menninger Foundation. Mark's professional career has been working in psychiatric hospitals in positions ranging from the delivery of clinical services to the director of marketing. He resides in Topeka, Kansas, with his wife Melissa and their three boys Aaron, Ryan and Charles. Mark has been a speaker and trainer with several national agencies, focusing on psychology and overall health.

The editor

Michael F. Ryan, editorial page editor of the Topeka Capital-Journal, is a 20-year journalist and, among other honors, has been cited for the best editorials in Kansas six times. He is a native of Prairie Village, Kansas, and graduated from Washburn University of Topeka before joining the McPherson Sentinel in 1981 and The Topeka Capital-Journal in 1983. He lives in Topeka with his wife, Susan, daughter Amanda and son Kevin.

The photographer

David Eulitt has been a staff photographer at The Topeka Capital-Journal since 1991. He graduated from the University of Missouri at Columbia in 1988 with a photojournalism degree. David was the 1993 winner of the Robert F. Kennedy Award for distinguished journalism for a photo essay on the 1992 Paralympic Games in Barcelona, Spain.

Prior to working in Topeka, Eulitt worked as a staff photographer at the San Bernardino California Sun for four years. He is married to Kelley Carpenter.

Photo Credits

The cover: Mark Hood
Chapter #1: Mark Hood
Chapter #2: Mark Hood
Chapter #3: Mark Hood
Chapter #4: Mark Hood
Chapter #5: Dave Eulitt
Chapter #6: Dave Eulitt
Chapter #7: Dave Eulitt
Chapter #8: Dave Eulitt
Chapter #9: Mark Hood
Chapter #10: Michael Ryan
Chapter #11: Dave Eulitt
Chapter #12: Mark Hood
Chapter #13: Dave Eulitt
Chapter #14: Dave Eulitt
Chapter #15: Dave Eulitt
Chapter #16: Dave Eulitt
Chapter #17: Michael Ryan
Epilogue: Marcia Slott
Back cover: Jane Hood (My mom)

The author on the road to the beginning

0-595-21944-6